Highway
Code
FOR MOTORCYCLISTS

© Haynes Publishing 2012

Pages 4–129 reproduced from *The Official Highway Code*. Department for Transport and Driving Standards Agency © Crown Copyright 2011. Reproduced under the terms of the Click-Use Licence

First published in February 2012

A catalogue record for this book is available from the British Library

ISBN 978 0 85733 152 6

Published by Haynes Publishing,
Sparkford, Yeovil, Somerset BA22 7JJ, UK

Tel: +44 (0)1963 442030 Fax: +44 (0)1963 440001
E-mail: sales@haynes.co.uk
Website: www.haynes.co.uk

Haynes North America, Inc.,
861 Lawrence Drive, Newbury Park,
California 91320, USA

Printed in the USA by Odcombe Press LP,
1299 Bridgestone Parkway, La Vergne, TN 37086

Contents

Introduction

This Highway Code applies to England, Scotland and Wales. *The Highway Code* is essential reading for everyone. The most vulnerable road users are pedestrians, particularly children, older or disabled people, cyclists, motorcyclists and horse riders. It is important that all road users are aware of the Code and are considerate towards each other. This applies to pedestrians as much as to drivers and riders.

Many of the rules in the Code are legal requirements, and if you disobey these rules you are committing a criminal offence. You may be fined, given penalty points on your licence or be disqualified from driving. In the most serious cases you may be sent to prison. Such rules are identified by the use of the words **'MUST/MUST NOT'**. In addition, the rule includes an abbreviated reference to the legislation which creates the offence. An explanation of the abbreviations is on page 118.

Although failure to comply with the other rules of the Code will not, in itself, cause a person to be prosecuted, *The Highway Code* may be used in evidence in any court proceedings under the Traffic Acts (see page 118) to establish liability. This includes rules which use advisory wording such as 'should/should not' or 'do/do not'.

Knowing and applying the rules contained in *The Highway Code* could significantly reduce road casualties. Cutting the number of deaths and injuries that occur on our roads every day is a responsibility we all share. *The Highway Code* can help us discharge that responsibility. Further information on driving/riding techniques can be found in 'The Official DSA Guide to Driving – the essential skills' and 'The Official DSA Guide to Riding – the essential skills'.

Rules for pedestrians

General guidance

1 **Pavements** (including any path along the side of a road) should be used if provided. Where possible, avoid being next to the kerb with your back to the traffic. If you have to step into the road, look both ways first. Always show due care and consideration for others.

2 **If there is no pavement,** keep to the right-hand side of the road so that you can see oncoming traffic. You should take extra care and

- be prepared to walk in single file, especially on narrow roads or in poor light
- keep close to the side of the road.

It may be safer to cross the road well before a sharp right-hand bend so that oncoming traffic has a better chance of seeing you. Cross back after the bend.

3 **Help other road users to see you.** Wear or carry something light-coloured, bright or fluorescent in poor daylight conditions. When it is dark, use reflective materials (e.g. armbands, sashes, waistcoats, jackets, footwear), which can be seen by drivers using headlights up to three times as far away as non-reflective materials.

Rule 3 *– Help yourself to be seen*

4 **Young children** should not be out alone on the pavement or road (see Rule 7). When taking children out, keep between them and the traffic and hold their hands firmly. Strap very young children into push-chairs or use reins. When pushing a young child in a buggy, do not push the buggy into the road when checking to see if it is clear to cross, particularly from between parked vehicles.

5 **Organised walks.** Large groups of people walking together should use a pavement if available; if one is not, they should keep to the left. Look-outs should be positioned at the front and back of the group, and they should wear fluorescent clothes in daylight and reflective clothes in the dark. At night, the look-out in front should show a white light and the one at the back a red light. People on the outside of large groups should also carry lights and wear reflective clothing.

6 **Motorways.** Pedestrians **MUST NOT** be on motorways or slip roads except in an emergency (see Rules 271 and 275).

Laws RTRA sect 17, MT(E&W)R 1982 as amended, reg 15(1)(b) & MT(S)R reg 13

Crossing the road

7 **The Green Cross Code.** The advice given below on crossing the road is for all pedestrians. Children should be taught the Code and should not be allowed out alone until they can understand and use it properly. The age when they can do this is different for each child. Many children cannot judge how fast vehicles are going or how far away they are. Children learn by example, so parents and carers should always use the Code in full when out with their children. They are responsible for deciding at what age children can use it safely by themselves.

A First find a safe place to cross and where there is space to reach the pavement on the other side. Where there is a crossing nearby, use it. It is safer to cross using a subway, a footbridge, an island, a zebra, pelican, toucan or puffin crossing, or where there is a crossing point controlled by a police officer, a school crossing patrol or a traffic warden. Otherwise choose a place where you can see clearly in all directions. Try to avoid crossing between parked cars (see Rule 14), on a blind bend, or close to the brow of a hill. Move to a space where drivers and riders can see you clearly. Do not cross the road diagonally.

Rule 7 – *Look all around and listen for traffic before crossing*

B Stop just before you get to the kerb, where you can see if anything is coming. Do not get too close to the traffic. If there's no pavement, keep back from the edge of the road but make sure you can still see approaching traffic.

C Look all around for traffic and listen. Traffic could come from any direction. Listen as well, because you can sometimes hear traffic before you see it.

D If traffic is coming, let it pass. Look all around again and listen. Do not cross until there is a safe gap in the traffic and you are certain that there is plenty of time. Remember, even if traffic is a long way off, it may be approaching very quickly.

E When it is safe, go straight across the road – do not run. Keep looking and listening for traffic while you cross, in case there is any traffic you did not see, or in case other traffic appears suddenly. Look out for cyclists and motorcyclists travelling between lanes of traffic. Do not walk diagonally across the road.

8 **At a junction.** When crossing the road, look out for traffic turning into the road, especially from behind you. If you have started crossing and traffic wants to turn into the road, you have priority and they should give way (see Rule 170).

9 **Pedestrian Safety Barriers.** Where there are barriers, cross the road only at the gaps provided for pedestrians. Do not climb over the barriers or walk between them and the road.

10 **Tactile paving.** Raised surfaces that can be felt underfoot provide warning and guidance to blind or partially sighted people. The most common surfaces are a series of raised studs, which are used at crossing points with a dropped kerb, or a series of rounded raised bars which are used at level crossings, at the top and bottom of steps and at some other hazards.

11 **One-way streets.** Check which way the traffic is moving. Do not cross until it is safe to do so without stopping. Bus and cycle lanes may operate in the opposite direction to the rest of the traffic.

12 **Bus and cycle lanes.** Take care when crossing these lanes as traffic may be moving faster than in the other lanes, or against the flow of traffic.

13 **Routes shared with cyclists.** Some cycle tracks run alongside footpaths or pavements, using a segregating feature to separate cyclists from people on foot. Segregated routes may also incorporate short lengths of tactile paving to help visually impaired people stay on the correct side. On the pedestrian side this will comprise a series of flat-topped bars running across the direction of travel (ladder pattern). On the cyclist side the same bars are orientated in the direction of travel (tramline pattern). Not all routes which are shared with cyclists are segregated. Take extra care where this is so (see Rule 62).

14 **Parked vehicles.** If you have to cross between parked vehicles, use the outside edges of the vehicles as if they were the kerb. Stop there and make sure you can see all around and that the traffic can see you. Make sure there is a gap between any parked vehicles on the other side, so you can reach the pavement. Never cross the road in front of, or behind, any vehicle with its engine running, especially a large vehicle, as the driver may not be able to see you.

15 **Reversing vehicles.** Never cross behind a vehicle which is reversing, showing white reversing lights or sounding a warning.

16 **Moving vehicles.** You **MUST NOT** get onto or hold onto a moving vehicle.
Law RTA 1988 sect 26

17 **At night.** Wear something reflective to make it easier for others to see you (see Rule 3). If there is no pedestrian crossing nearby, cross the road near a street light so that traffic can see you more easily.

Crossings

18 **At all crossings.** When using any type of crossing you should

- ⊘ always check that the traffic has stopped before you start to cross or push a pram onto a crossing
- ⊘ always cross between the studs or over the zebra markings. Do not cross at the side of the crossing or on the zig-zag lines, as it can be dangerous.

You **MUST NOT** loiter on any type of crossing.
Laws ZPPPCRGD reg 19 & RTRA sect 25(5)

19 **Zebra crossings.** Give traffic plenty of time to see you and to stop before you start to cross. Vehicles will need more time when the road is slippery. Wait until traffic has stopped from both directions or the road is clear before crossing. Remember that traffic does not have to stop until someone has moved onto the crossing. Keep looking both ways, and listening, in case a driver or rider has not seen you and attempts to overtake a vehicle that has stopped.

Rule 19 – *Zebra crossings have flashing beacons*

20 Where there is an island in the middle of a zebra crossing, wait on the island and follow Rule 19 before you cross the second half of the road – it is a separate crossing.

Rule 20 *– Zebra crossings with a central island are two separate crossings*

21 **At traffic lights.** There may be special signals for pedestrians. You should only start to cross the road when the green figure shows. If you have started to cross the road and the green figure goes out, you should still have time to reach the other side, but do not delay. If no pedestrian signals have been provided, watch carefully and do not cross until the traffic lights are red and the traffic has stopped. Keep looking and check for traffic that may be turning the corner. Remember that traffic lights may let traffic move in some lanes while traffic in other lanes has stopped.

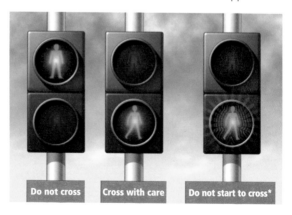

Do not cross   Cross with care   Do not start to cross*

Rule 21 *– At traffic lights, puffin and pelican crossings*
* At pelican crossings only

22 **Pelican crossings.** These are signal-controlled crossings operated by pedestrians. Push the control button to activate the traffic signals. When the red figure shows, do not cross. When a steady green figure shows, check the traffic has stopped then cross with care. When the green figure begins to flash you should not start to cross. If you have already started you should have time to finish crossing safely.

23 **Puffin crossings** differ from pelican crossings as the red and green figures are above the control box on your side of the road and there is no flashing green figure phase. Press the button and wait for the green figure to show.

24 When the road is congested, traffic on your side of the road may be forced to stop even though their lights are green. Traffic may still be moving on the other side of the road, so press the button and wait for the signal to cross.

25 **Toucan crossings** are light-controlled crossings which allow cyclists and pedestrians to share crossing space and cross at the same time. They are push-button operated. Pedestrians and cyclists will see the green signal together. Cyclists are permitted to ride across.

Rule 25 *– Toucan crossings can be used by both cyclists and pedestrians*

26 At some crossings there is a bleeping sound or voice signal to indicate to blind or partially sighted people when the steady green figure is showing, and there may be a tactile signal to help deafblind people.

27 **Equestrian crossings** are for horse riders. They have pavement barriers, wider crossing spaces, horse and rider figures in the light panels and either two sets of controls (one higher), or just one higher control panel.

Rule 27 – *Equestrian crossings are used by horse riders. There is often a parallel crossing*

28 **'Staggered' pelican or puffin crossings.** When the crossings on each side of the central refuge are not in line are two separate crossings. On reaching the central island, press the button again and wait for a steady green figure.

Rule 28 – *Staggered crossings (with an island in the middle) are two separate crossings*

29 **Crossings controlled by an authorised person.** Do not cross the road unless you are signalled to do so by a police officer, traffic warden or school crossing patrol. Always cross in front of them.

30 Where there are no controlled crossing points available it is advisable to cross where there is an island in the middle of the road. Use the Green Cross Code (see Rule 7) to cross to the island and then stop and use it again to cross the second half of the road.

Situations needing extra care

31 **Emergency vehicles.** If an ambulance, fire engine, police or other emergency vehicle approaches using flashing blue lights, headlights and/or sirens, keep off the road.

32 **Buses.** Get on or off a bus only when it has stopped to allow you to do so. Watch out for cyclists when you are getting off. Never cross the road directly behind or in front of a bus. Wait until it has moved off and you can see clearly in both directions.

33 **Tramways.** These may run through pedestrian areas. Their path will be marked out by shallow kerbs, changes in the paving or other road surface, white lines or yellow dots. Cross at designated crossings where provided. Elsewhere treat trams as you would other road vehicles and look both ways along the track before crossing. Do not walk along the track as trams may come up behind you. Trams move quietly and cannot steer to avoid you.

34 **Railway level crossings.** You **MUST NOT** cross or pass a stop line when the red lights show, (including a red pedestrian figure). Also do not cross if an alarm is sounding or the barriers are being lowered. The tone of the alarm may change if another train is approaching. If there are no lights, alarms or barriers, stop, look both ways and listen before crossing. A tactile surface comprising rounded bars running across the direction of pedestrian travel may be installed on the footpath approaching a level crossing to warn visually impaired people of its presence. The tactile surface should extend across the full width of the footway and should be located at an appropriate distance from the barrier or projected line of the barrier.

Law TSRGD, reg 52

35 **Street and pavement repairs.** A pavement may be closed temporarily because it is not safe to use. Take extra care if you are directed to walk in or to cross the road.

Rules for users of powered wheelchairs and powered mobility scooters

(called Invalid Carriages in law)

36 There is one class of manual wheelchair (called a Class 1 invalid carriage) and two classes of powered wheelchairs and powered mobility scooters. Manual wheelchairs and Class 2 vehicles are those with an upper speed limit of 4 mph (6 km/h) and are designed to be used on pavements. Class 3 vehicles are those with an upper speed limit of 8 mph (12 km/h) and are equipped to be used on the road as well as the pavement.

37 When you are on the road you should obey the guidance and rules for other vehicles; when on the pavement you should follow the guidance and rules for pedestrians.

On pavements

38 Pavements are safer than roads and should be used when available. You should give pedestrians priority and show consideration for other pavement users, particularly those with a hearing or visual impairment who may not be aware that you are there.

39 Powered wheelchairs and scooters **MUST NOT** travel faster than 4 mph (6 km/h) on pavements or in pedestrian areas. You may need to reduce your speed to adjust to other pavement users who may not be able to move out of your way quickly enough or where the pavement is too narrow.

Law UICHR 1988 reg 4

40 When moving off the pavement onto the road, you should take special care. Before moving off, always look round and make sure it's safe to join the traffic. Always try to use dropped kerbs when moving off the pavement, even if this means travelling further to locate one. If you have to climb or descend a kerb, always approach it at right angles and don't try to negotiate a kerb higher than the vehicle manufacturer's recommendations.

On the road

41 You should take care when travelling on the road as you may be travelling more slowly than other traffic (your machine is restricted to 8 mph (12 km/h) and may be less visible).

42 When on the road, Class 3 vehicles should travel in the direction of the traffic. Class 2 users should always use the pavement when it is available. When there is no pavement, you should use caution when on the road. Class 2 users should, where possible, travel in the direction of the traffic. If you are travelling at night when lights **MUST** be used, you should travel in the direction of the traffic to avoid confusing other road users.

Law UICHR 1988 reg 9

43 You **MUST** follow the same rules about using lights, indicators and horns as for other road vehicles, if your vehicle is fitted with them. At night, lights **MUST** be used. Be aware that other road users may not see you and you should make yourself more visible – even in the daytime and also at dusk – by, for instance, wearing a reflective jacket or reflective strips on the back of the vehicle.

Law UICHR 1988 reg 9

44 Take extra care at road junctions. When going straight ahead, check to make sure there are no vehicles about to cross your path from the left, the right, or overtaking you and turning left. There are several options for dealing with right turns, especially turning from a major road. If moving into the middle of the road is difficult or dangerous, you can

- ○ stop on the left-hand side of the road and wait for a safe gap in the traffic
- ○ negotiate the turn as a pedestrian, i.e. travel along the pavement and cross the road between pavements where it is safe to do so. Class 3 users should switch the vehicle to the lower speed limit when on pavements.

If the junction is too hazardous, it may be worth considering an alternative route. Similarly, when negotiating major roundabouts (i.e. with two or more lanes) it may be safer for you to use the pavement or find a route which avoids the roundabout altogether.

45 All normal parking restrictions should be observed. Your vehicle should not be left unattended if it causes an obstruction to other pedestrians – especially those in wheelchairs. Parking concessions provided under the Blue Badge scheme (see page 129) will apply to those vehicles displaying a valid badge.

46 These vehicles **MUST NOT** be used on motorways (see Rule 253). They should not be used on unrestricted dual carriageways where the speed limit exceeds 50 mph (80 km/h) but if they are used on these dual carriageways, they **MUST** have a flashing amber beacon. A flashing amber beacon should be used on all other dual carriageways (see Rule 220).

Laws RTRA sect 17(2) & (3), & RVLR reg 17(1) & 26

Rules about animals

Horse-drawn vehicles

47 Horse-drawn vehicles used on the highway should be operated and maintained in accordance with standards set out in the Department for Transport's Code of Practice for Horse-Drawn Vehicles. This Code lays down the requirements for a road driving assessment and includes a comprehensive list of safety checks to ensure that a carriage and its fittings are safe and in good working order. The standards set out in the Road Driving Assessment may be required to be met by a Local Authority if an operator wishes to obtain a local authority licence to operate a passenger-carrying service (see page 129).

48 **Safety equipment and clothing.** All horse-drawn vehicles should have two red rear reflectors. It is safer not to drive at night but if you do, a light showing white to the front and red to the rear **MUST** be fitted.

Law RVLR 1989 reg 4

Horse riders

49 **Safety equipment.** Children under the age of 14 **MUST** wear a helmet which complies with the Regulations. It **MUST** be fastened securely. Other riders should also follow these requirements. These requirements do not apply to a child who is a follower of the Sikh religion while wearing a turban.

Laws H(PHYR) Act 1990, sect 1 & H(PHYR) Regulations 1992, reg 3

50 **Other clothing.** You should wear

- boots or shoes with hard soles and heels
- light-coloured or fluorescent clothing in daylight
- reflective clothing if you have to ride at night or in poor visibility.

Rule 50 – *Help yourself to be seen*

51 **At night.** It is safer not to ride on the road at night or in poor visibility, but if you do, make sure you wear reflective clothing and your horse has reflective bands above the fetlock joints. A light which shows white to the front and red to the rear should be fitted, with a band, to the rider's right arm and/or leg/riding boot. If you are leading a horse at night, carry a light in your right hand, showing white to the front and red to the rear, and wear reflective clothing on both you and your horse. It is strongly recommended that a fluorescent/reflective tail guard is also worn by your horse.

Riding

52 Before you take a horse on to a road, you should

⊙ ensure all tack fits well and is in good condition
⊙ make sure you can control the horse.

Always ride with other, less nervous horses if you think that your horse will be nervous of traffic.
Never ride a horse without both a saddle and bridle.

53 Before riding off or turning, look behind you to make sure it is safe, then give a clear arm signal.

When riding on the road you should
⊙ keep to the left
⊙ keep both hands on the reins unless you are signalling
⊙ keep both feet in the stirrups
⊙ not carry another person

- not carry anything which might affect your balance or get tangled up with the reins
- keep a horse you are leading to your left
- move in the direction of the traffic flow in a one-way street
- never ride more than two abreast, and ride in single file on narrow or busy roads and when riding round bends.

54 You **MUST NOT** take a horse onto a footpath or pavement, and you should not take a horse onto a cycle track. Use a bridleway where possible. Equestrian crossings may be provided for horse riders to cross the road and you should use these where available (see page 12). You should dismount at level crossings where a 'horse rider dismount' sign is displayed.

Laws HA 1835 sect 72, R(S)A 1984, sect 129(5)

55 Avoid roundabouts wherever possible. If you use them you should

- keep to the left and watch out for vehicles crossing your path to leave or join the roundabout
- signal right when riding across exits to show you are not leaving
- signal left just before you leave the roundabout.

Other animals

56 **Dogs.** Do not let a dog out on the road on its own. Keep it on a short lead when walking on the pavement, road or path shared with cyclists or horse riders.

57 When in a vehicle make sure dogs or other animals are suitably restrained so they cannot distract you while you are driving or injure you, or themselves, if you stop quickly. A seat belt harness, pet carrier, dog cage or dog guard are ways of restraining animals in cars.

58 **Animals being herded.** These should be kept under control at all times. You should, if possible, send another person along the road in front to warn other road users, especially at a bend or the brow of a hill. It is safer not to move animals after dark, but if you do, then wear reflective clothing and ensure that lights are carried (white at the front and red at the rear of the herd).

Rules for cyclists

These rules are in addition to those in the following sections, which apply to all vehicles (except the motorway section on page 85). See also page 112 – You and your bicycle.

59 **Clothing.** You should wear

- ⊘ a cycle helmet which conforms to current regulations, is the correct size and securely fastened
- ⊘ appropriate clothes for cycling. Avoid clothes which may get tangled in the chain, or in a wheel or may obscure your lights
- ⊘ light-coloured or fluorescent clothing which helps other road users to see you in daylight and poor light
- ⊘ reflective clothing and/or accessories (belt, arm or ankle bands) in the dark.

Rule 59 – Help yourself to be seen

60 **At night** your cycle **MUST** have white front and red rear lights lit. It **MUST** also be fitted with a red rear reflector (and amber pedal reflectors, if manufactured after 1/10/85). White front reflectors and spoke reflectors will also help you to be seen. Flashing lights are permitted but it is recommended that cyclists who are riding in areas without street lighting use a steady front lamp.

Law RVLR regs 13, 18 & 24

61 **Cycle Routes and Other Facilities.** Use cycle routes, advanced stop lines, cycle boxes and toucan crossings unless at the time it is unsafe to do so. Use of these facilities is not compulsory and will depend on your experience and skills, but they can make your journey safer.

62 **Cycle Tracks.** These are normally located away from the road, but may occasionally be found alongside footpaths or pavements. Cyclists and pedestrians may be segregated or they may share the same space (unsegregated). When using segregated tracks you **MUST** keep to the side intended for cyclists as the pedestrian side remains a pavement or footpath. Take care when passing pedestrians, especially children, older or disabled people, and allow them plenty of room. Always be prepared to slow down and stop if necessary. Take care near road junctions as you may have difficulty seeing other road users, who might not notice you.
Law HA 1835 sect 72

63 **Cycle Lanes.** These are marked by a white line (which may be broken) along the carriageway (see Rule 140). Keep within the lane when practicable. When leaving a cycle lane check before pulling out that it is safe to do so and signal your intention clearly to other road users. Use of cycle lanes is not compulsory and will depend on your experience and skills, but they can make your journey safer.

64 You **MUST NOT** cycle on a pavement.
Laws HA 1835 sect 72 & R(S)A 1984, sect 129

65 **Bus Lanes.** Most bus lanes may be used by cyclists as indicated on signs. Watch out for people getting on or off a bus. Be very careful when overtaking a bus or leaving a bus lane as you will be entering a busier traffic flow. Do not pass between the kerb and a bus when it is at a stop.

66 You should

- ↻ keep both hands on the handlebars except when signalling or changing gear
- ↻ keep both feet on the pedals
- ↻ never ride more than two abreast, and ride in single file on narrow or busy roads and when riding round bends
- ↻ not ride close behind another vehicle
- ↻ not carry anything which will affect your balance or may get tangled up with your wheels or chain
- ↻ be considerate of other road users, particularly blind and partially sighted pedestrians. Let them know you are there when necessary, for example, by ringing your bell if you have one. It is recommended that a bell be fitted.

67 You should

- ↻ look all around before moving away from the kerb, turning or manoeuvring, to make sure it is safe to do so. Give a clear signal to show other road users what you intend to do (see page 97)
- ↻ look well ahead for obstructions in the road, such as drains, pot-holes and parked vehicles so that you do not have to swerve suddenly to avoid them. Leave plenty of room when passing parked vehicles and watch out for doors being opened or pedestrians stepping into your path
- ↻ be aware of traffic coming up behind you
- ↻ take extra care near road humps, narrowings and other traffic calming features
- ↻ take care when overtaking (see Rules 162–169).

68 You MUST NOT

- ↻ carry a passenger unless your cycle has been built or adapted to carry one
- ↻ hold onto a moving vehicle or trailer
- ↻ ride in a dangerous, careless or inconsiderate manner
- ↻ ride when under the influence of drink or drugs, including medicine.

Law RTA 1988 sects 24, 26, 28, 29 & 30 as amended by RTA 1991

69 You MUST obey all traffic signs and traffic light signals.

Laws RTA 1988 sect 36 & TSRGD reg 10(1)

70 When parking your cycle

- ↻ find a conspicuous location where it can be seen by passers-by
- ↻ use cycle stands or other cycle parking facilities wherever possible
- ↻ do not leave it where it would cause an obstruction or hazard to other road users
- ↻ secure it well so that it will not fall over and become an obstruction or hazard.

71 You **MUST NOT** cross the stop line when the traffic lights are red. Some junctions have an advanced stop line to enable you to wait and position yourself ahead of other traffic (see Rule 178).

Laws RTA 1988 sect 36 & TSRGD regs 10 & 36(1)

Road junctions

72 **On the left.** When approaching a junction on the left, watch out for vehicles turning in front of you, out of or into the side road. Just before you turn, check for undertaking cyclists or motorcyclists. Do not ride on the inside of vehicles signalling or slowing down to turn left.

73 Pay particular attention to long vehicles which need a lot of room to manoeuvre at corners. Be aware that drivers may not see you. They may have to move over to the right before turning left. Wait until they have completed the manoeuvre because the rear wheels come very close to the kerb while turning. Do not be tempted to ride in the space between them and the kerb.

74 **On the right.** If you are turning right, check the traffic to ensure it is safe, then signal and move to the centre of the road. Wait until there is a safe gap in the oncoming traffic and give a final look before completing the turn. It may be safer to wait on the left until there is a safe gap or to dismount and push your cycle across the road.

75 **Dual carriageways.** Remember that traffic on most dual carriageways moves quickly. When crossing wait for a safe gap and cross each carriageway in turn. Take extra care when crossing slip roads.

23

76 ### Roundabouts
Full details about the correct procedure at roundabouts are contained in Rules 184–190. Roundabouts can be hazardous and should be approached with care.

77 You may feel safer walking your cycle round on the pavement or verge. If you decide to ride round keeping to the left-hand lane you should

- be aware that drivers may not easily see you
- take extra care when cycling across exits. You may need to signal right to show you are not leaving the roundabout
- watch out for vehicles crossing your path to leave or join the roundabout.

78 Give plenty of room to long vehicles on the roundabout as they need more space to manoeuvre. Do not ride in the space they need to get round the roundabout. It may be safer to wait until they have cleared the roundabout.

Crossing the road
79 Do not ride across equestrian crossings, as they are for horse riders only. Do not ride across a pelican, puffin or zebra crossing. Dismount and wheel your cycle across.

80 **Toucan crossings.** These are light-controlled crossings which allow cyclists and pedestrians to share crossing space and cross at the same time. They are push-button operated. Pedestrians and cyclists will see the green signal together. Cyclists are permitted to ride across.

81 **Cycle-only crossings.** Cycle tracks on opposite sides of the road may be linked by signalled crossings. You may ride across but you **MUST NOT** cross until the green cycle symbol is showing.
Law TSRGD regs 33(2) & 36(1)

82 **Level crossings/Tramways.** Take extra care when crossing the tracks (see Rule 306). You should dismount at level crossings where a 'cyclist dismount' sign is displayed.

Rules for motorcyclists

These Rules are in addition to those in the following sections which apply to all vehicles. For motorcycle licence requirements see pages 112–114.

General

83 On all journeys, the rider and pillion passenger on a motorcycle, scooter or moped **MUST** wear a protective helmet. This does not apply to a follower of the Sikh religion while wearing a turban. Helmets **MUST** comply with the Regulations and they **MUST** be fastened securely. Riders and passengers of motor tricycles and quadricycles, also called quadbikes, should also wear a protective helmet. Before each journey check that your helmet visor is clean and in good condition.
Laws RTA 1988 sects 16 & 17 & MC(PH)R as amended reg 4

84 It is also advisable to wear eye protectors, which **MUST** comply with the Regulations. Scratched or poorly fitting eye protectors can limit your view when riding, particularly in bright sunshine and the hours of darkness. Consider wearing ear protection. Strong boots, gloves and suitable clothing may help to protect you if you are involved in a collision.
Laws RTA sect 18 & MC(EP)R as amended reg 4

85 You **MUST NOT** carry more than one pillion passenger who **MUST** sit astride the machine on a proper seat. They should face forward with both feet on the footrests. You **MUST NOT** carry a pillion passenger unless your motor cycle is designed to do so. Provisional licence holders **MUST NOT** carry a pillion passenger.
Laws RTA 1988 sect 23, MV(DL)R 1999 reg 16(6) & CUR 1986 reg 102

86 **Daylight riding.** Make yourself as visible as possible from the side as well as the front and rear. You could wear a light or brightly coloured helmet and fluorescent clothing or strips. Dipped headlights, even in good daylight, may also make you more conspicuous. However, be aware that other vehicle drivers may still not have seen you, or judged your distance or speed correctly, especially at junctions.

***Rule 86** – Help yourself to be seen*

87 **Riding in the dark.** Wear reflective clothing or strips to improve your visibility in the dark. These reflect light from the headlamps of other vehicles, making you visible from a longer distance. See Rules113–116 for lighting requirements.

88 **Manoeuvring.** You should be aware of what is behind and to the sides before manoeuvring. Look behind you; use mirrors if they are fitted. When in traffic queues look out for pedestrians crossing between vehicles and vehicles emerging from junctions or changing lanes. Position yourself so that drivers in front can see you in their mirrors. Additionally, when filtering in slow-moving traffic, take care and keep your speed low.

Remember:
Observation – Signal – Manoeuvre.

Rules for drivers and motorcyclists

89 **Vehicle condition.** You **MUST** ensure your vehicle and trailer comply with the full requirements of the Road Vehicles (Construction and Use) Regulations and Road Vehicles Lighting Regulations (see page 118).

Fitness to drive

90 Make sure that you are fit to drive. You **MUST** report to the Driver and Vehicle Licensing Agency (DVLA) any health condition likely to affect your driving.
Law RTA 1988 sect 94

91 Driving when you are tired greatly increases your risk of collision. To minimise this risk

- make sure you are fit to drive. Do not begin a journey if you are tired. Get a good night's sleep before embarking on a long journey
- avoid undertaking long journeys between midnight and 6 am, when natural alertness is at a minimum
- plan your journey to take sufficient breaks. A minimum break of at least 15 minutes after every two hours of driving is recommended
- if you feel at all sleepy, stop in a safe place. Do not stop on the hard shoulder of a motorway
- the most effective ways to counter sleepiness are to drink, for example, two cups of caffeinated coffee and to take a short nap (at least 15 minutes).

92 **Vision.** You **MUST** be able to read a vehicle number plate, in good daylight, from a distance of 20 metres (or 20.5 metres where the old style number plate is used). If you need to wear glasses (or contact lenses) to do this, you **MUST** wear them at all times while driving. The police have the power to require a driver to undertake an eyesight test.
Laws RTA 1988 sect 96 & MV(DL)R reg 40 & sch 8

93 Slow down, and if necessary stop, if you are dazzled by bright sunlight.

94 At night or in poor visibility, do not use tinted glasses, lenses or visors if they restrict your vision.

Alcohol and drugs

95 **Do not drink and drive** as it will seriously affect your judgement and abilities. You **MUST NOT** drive with a breath alcohol level higher than 35 microgrammes/100 millilitres of breath or a blood alcohol level of more than 80 milligrammes/100 millilitres of blood. Alcohol will

- give a false sense of confidence
- reduce co-ordination and slow down reactions
- affect judgement of speed, distance and risk
- reduce your driving ability, even if you're below the legal limit
- take time to leave your body; you may be unfit to drive in the evening after drinking at lunchtime, or in the morning after drinking the previous evening.

The best solution is not to drink at all when planning to drive because any amount of alcohol affects your ability to drive safely. If you are going to drink, arrange another means of transport.

Law RTA 1988 sects 4, 5 & 11(2)

96 You **MUST NOT** drive under the influence of drugs or medicine. Check the instructions or ask your doctor or pharmacist. Using illegal drugs is highly dangerous. Never take them if you intend to drive; the effects are unpredictable, but can be even more severe than alcohol and may result in fatal or serious road crashes.

Law RTA 1988 sect 4

97 **Before setting off.** You should ensure that

- you have planned your route and allowed sufficient time
- clothing and footwear do not prevent you using the controls in the correct manner
- you know where all the controls are and how to use them before you need them. Not all vehicles are the same; do not wait until it is too late to find out
- your mirrors and seat are adjusted correctly to ensure comfort, full control and maximum vision
- head restraints are properly adjusted to reduce the risk of neck and spine injuries in the event of a collision
- you have sufficient fuel before commencing your journey, especially if it includes motorway driving. It can be dangerous to lose power when driving in traffic
- ensure your vehicle is legal and roadworthy
- switch off your mobile phone.

Rule 97 *– Make sure head restraints are properly adjusted*

98 **Vehicle towing and loading.** As a driver

- you **MUST NOT** tow more than your licence permits. If you passed a car test after 1 Jan 1997 you are restricted on the weight of trailer you can tow
- you **MUST NOT** overload your vehicle or trailer. You should not tow a weight greater than that recommended by the manufacturer of your vehicle
- you **MUST** secure your load and it **MUST NOT** stick out dangerously. Make sure any heavy or sharp objects and any animals are secured safely. If there is a collision, they might hit someone inside the vehicle and cause serious injury
- you should properly distribute the weight in your caravan or trailer with heavy items mainly over the axle(s) and ensure a downward load on the tow ball. Manufacturer's recommended weight and tow ball load should not be exceeded. This should avoid the possibility of swerving or snaking and going out of control. If this does happen, ease off the accelerator and reduce speed gently to regain control
- carrying a load or pulling a trailer may require you to adjust the headlights.

In the event of a breakdown, be aware that towing a vehicle on a tow rope is potentially dangerous. You should consider professional recovery.

Laws CUR reg 100 & MV(DL)R reg 43

Seat belts and child restraints

99 You **MUST** wear a seat belt in cars, vans and other goods vehicles if one is fitted (see table below). Adults, and children aged 14 years and over, **MUST** use a seat belt or child restraint, where fitted, when seated in minibuses, buses and coaches. Exemptions are allowed for the holders of medical exemption certificates and those making deliveries or collections in goods vehicles when travelling less than 50 metres (approx 162 feet).

Laws RTA 1988 sects 14 & 15, MV(WSB)R, MV(WSBCFS)R & MV(WSB)(A)R

Seat belt requirements. This table summarises the main legal requirements for wearing seat belts in cars, vans and other goods vehicles

	Front seat	Rear seat	Who is responsible?
Driver	Seat belt **MUST** be worn if fitted		**Driver**
Child under 3 years of age	Correct child restraint **MUST** be used	Correct child restraint **MUST** be used. If one is not available in a taxi, may travel unrestrained.	**Driver**
Child from 3rd birthday up to 1.35 metres in height (or 12th birthday, whichever they reach first)	Correct child restraint **MUST** be used	Correct child restraint **MUST** be used where seat belts fitted. **MUST** use adult belt if correct child restraint is not available in a licensed taxi or private hire vehicle, or for reasons of unexpected necessity over a short distance, or if two occupied restraints prevent fitment of a third.	**Driver**
Child over 1.35 metres (approx 4ft 5ins) in height or 12 or 13 years	Adult seat belt **MUST** be worn if available	Adult seat belt **MUST** be worn if available	**Driver**
Adult passengers aged 14 and over	Seat belt **MUST** be worn if available	Seat belt **MUST** be worn if available	**Passenger**

Rule 100 – *Make sure that a child uses a suitable restraint which is correctly adjusted*

100 The driver **MUST** ensure that all children under 14 years of age in cars, vans and other goods vehicles wear seat belts or sit in an approved child restraint where required (see table above). If a child is under 1.35 metres (approx 4 feet 5 inches) tall, a baby seat, child seat, booster seat or booster cushion **MUST** be used suitable for the child's weight and fitted to the manufacturer's instructions.
Laws RTA 1988 sects 14 & 15, MV(WSB)R, MV(WSBCFS)R & MV(WSB)(A)R

101 A rear-facing baby seat **MUST NOT** be fitted into a seat protected by an active frontal airbag, as in a crash it can cause serious injury or death to the child.
Laws RTA 1988 sects 14 & 15, MV(WSB)R, MV(WSBCFS)R & MV(WSB)(A)R

102 **Children in cars, vans and other goods vehicles.** Drivers who are carrying children in cars, vans and other goods vehicles should also ensure that

- ⮩ children should get into the vehicle through the door nearest the kerb
- ⮩ child restraints are properly fitted to manufacturer's instructions
- ⮩ children do not sit behind the rear seats in an estate car or hatchback, unless a special child seat has been fitted
- ⮩ the child safety door locks, where fitted, are used when children are in the vehicle
- ⮩ children are kept under control.

General rules, techniques and advice for all drivers and riders

This section should be read by all drivers, motorcyclists, cyclists and horse riders. The rules in *The Highway Code* do not give you the right of way in any circumstance, but they advise you when you should give way to others. Always give way if it can help to avoid an incident.

Signals

103 Signals warn and inform other road users, including pedestrians (see page 97), of your intended actions. You should always

- give clear signals in plenty of time, having checked it is not misleading to signal at that time
- use them to advise other road users before changing course or direction, stopping or moving off
- cancel them after use
- make sure your signals will not confuse others. If, for instance, you want to stop after a side road, do not signal until you are passing the road. If you signal earlier it may give the impression that you intend to turn into the road. Your brake lights will warn traffic behind you that you are slowing down
- use an arm signal to emphasise or reinforce your signal if necessary. Remember that signalling does not give you priority.

104 You should also
- watch out for signals given by other road users and proceed only when you are satisfied that it is safe
- be aware that an indicator on another vehicle may not have been cancelled.

105 You **MUST** obey signals given by police officers, traffic officers, traffic wardens (see pages 104-105) and signs used by school crossing patrols.

Laws RTRA sect 28, RTA 1988 sect 35, TMA 2004 sect 6, & FTWO art 3

Police stopping procedures. If the police want to stop your vehicle they will, where possible, attract your attention by

- ➲ flashing blue lights, headlights or sounding their siren or horn, usually from behind
- ➲ directing you to pull over to the side by pointing and/or using the left indicator.

You **MUST** then pull over and stop as soon as it is safe to do so. Then switch off your engine.

Law RTA 1988 sect 163

Other stopping procedures

Vehicle & Operator Services Agency Officers have powers to stop vehicles on all roads, including motorways and trunk roads, in England and Wales. They will attract your attention by flashing amber lights

- ➲ either from the front requesting you to follow them to a safe place to stop
- ➲ or from behind directing you to pull over to the side by pointing and/or using the left indicator.

It is an offence not to comply with their directions. You **MUST** obey any signals given (see page 99).

Laws RTA 1988, sect 67, & PRA 2002, sect 41 & sched 5(8)

Highways Agency Traffic Officers have powers to stop vehicles on most motorways and some 'A' class roads, in England only. If HA traffic officers in uniform want to stop your vehicle on safety grounds (e.g. an insecure load) they will, where possible, attract your attention by

- ➲ flashing amber lights, usually from behind
- ➲ directing you to pull over to the side by pointing and/or using the left indicator.

You **MUST** then pull over and stop as soon as it is safe to do so. Then switch off your engine. It is an offence not to comply with their directions (see page 99).

Law RTA1988, sects 35 &163 as amended by TMA 2004, sect 6

109 **Traffic light signals and traffic signs.** You **MUST** obey all traffic light signals (see page 96) and traffic signs giving orders, including temporary signals & signs (see pages 100–107). Make sure you know, understand and act on all other traffic and information signs and road markings (see pages 100–111).

Laws RTA 1988 sect 36 & TSRGD regs 10, 15, 16, 25, 26, 27, 28, 29, 36, 38 & 40

110 **Flashing headlights.** Only flash your headlights to let other road users know that you are there. Do not flash your headlights to convey any other message or intimidate other road users.

111 Never assume that flashing headlights is a signal inviting you to proceed. Use your own judgement and proceed carefully.

112 **The horn.** Use only while your vehicle is moving and you need to warn other road users of your presence. Never sound your horn aggressively. You **MUST NOT** use your horn

- while stationary on the road
- when driving in a built-up area between the hours of 11.30 pm and 7.00 am

except when another road user poses a danger.

Law CUR reg 99

Lighting requirements

113 **You MUST**

- ensure all sidelights and rear registration plate lights are lit between sunset and sunrise
- use headlights at night, except on a road which has lit street lighting. These roads are generally restricted to a speed limit of 30 mph (48 km/h) unless otherwise specified
- use headlights when visibility is seriously reduced (see Rule 226).

Night (the hours of darkness) is defined as the period between half an hour after sunset and half an hour before sunrise.

Laws RVLR regs 3, 24, & 25, (In Scotland – RTRA 1984 sect 82 (as amended by NRSWA, para 59 of sched 8))

114

You MUST NOT

- ↻ use any lights in a way which would dazzle or cause discomfort to other road users, including pedestrians, cyclists and horse riders
- ↻ use front or rear fog lights unless visibility is seriously reduced. You **MUST** switch them off when visibility improves to avoid dazzling other road users (see Rule 226).

In stationary queues of traffic, drivers should apply the parking brake and, once the following traffic has stopped, take their foot off the footbrake to deactivate the vehicle brake lights. This will minimise glare to road users behind until the traffic moves again.

Law RVLR reg 27

115

You should also

- ↻ use dipped headlights, or dim-dip if fitted, at night in built-up areas and in dull daytime weather, to ensure that you can be seen
- ↻ keep your headlights dipped when overtaking until you are level with the other vehicle and then change to main beam if necessary, unless this would dazzle oncoming road users
- ↻ slow down, and if necessary stop, if you are dazzled by oncoming headlights.

116

Hazard warning lights. These may be used when your vehicle is stationary, to warn that it is temporarily obstructing traffic. Never use them as an excuse for dangerous or illegal parking. You **MUST NOT** use hazard warning lights while driving or being towed unless you are on a motorway or unrestricted dual carriageway and you need to warn drivers behind you of a hazard or obstruction ahead. Only use them for long enough to ensure that your warning has been observed.

Law RVLR reg 27

Control of the vehicle

Braking

117

In normal circumstances. The safest way to brake is to do so early and lightly. Brake more firmly as you begin to stop. Ease the pressure off just before the vehicle comes to rest to avoid a jerky stop.

118 **In an emergency.** Brake immediately. Try to avoid braking so harshly that you lock your wheels. Locked wheels can lead to loss of control.

119 **Skids.** Skidding is usually caused by the driver braking, accelerating or steering too harshly or driving too fast for the road conditions. If skidding occurs, remove the cause by releasing the brake pedal fully or easing off the accelerator. Turn the steering wheel in the direction of the skid. For example, if the rear of the vehicle skids to the right, steer immediately to the right to recover.

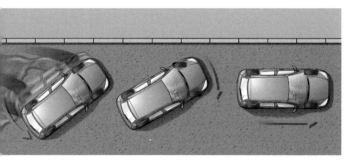

Rule 119 – *Rear of the car skids to the right. Driver steers to the right*

120 **ABS.** If your vehicle is fitted with anti-lock brakes, you should follow the advice given in the vehicle handbook. However, in the case of an emergency, apply the footbrake firmly; do not release the pressure until the vehicle has slowed to the desired speed. The ABS should ensure that steering control will be retained, but do not assume that a vehicle with ABS will stop in a shorter distance.

121 **Brakes affected by water.** If you have driven through deep water your brakes may be less effective. Test them at the first safe opportunity by pushing gently on the brake pedal to make sure that they work. If they are not fully effective, gently apply light pressure while driving slowly. This will help to dry them out.

122 **Coasting.** This term describes a vehicle travelling in neutral or with the clutch pressed down. It can reduce driver control because

- ◯ engine braking is eliminated
- ◯ vehicle speed downhill will increase quickly
- ◯ increased use of the footbrake can reduce its effectiveness
- ◯ steering response will be affected, particularly on bends and corners
- ◯ it may be more difficult to select the appropriate gear when needed.

123 **The Driver and the Environment.** You **MUST NOT** leave a parked vehicle unattended with the engine running or leave a vehicle engine running unnecessarily while that vehicle is stationary on a public road. Generally, if the vehicle is stationary and is likely to remain so for more than a couple of minutes, you should apply the parking brake and switch off the engine to reduce emissions and noise pollution. However it is permissible to leave the engine running if the vehicle is stationary in traffic or for diagnosing faults.

Law CUR regs 98 & 107

Speed Limits

Type of vehicle	Built-up areas* mph (km/h)	Single carriageways mph (km/h)	Double carriageways mph (km/h)	Motorways mph (km/h)
Cars & motorcycles (including car-derived vans up to 2 tonnes maximum laden weight)	30 (48)	60 (96)	70 (112)	70 (112)
Cars towing caravans or trailers (including car-derived vans and motorcycles)	30 (48)	50 (80)	60 (96)	60 (96)
Buses, coaches and minibuses (not exceeding 12 metres in overall length)	30 (48)	50 (80)	60 (96)	70** (112)
Goods vehicles (not exceeding 7.5 tonnes maximum laden weight)	30 (48)	50 (80)	60 (96)	70 (112)
Goods vehicles (exceeding 7.5 tonnes maximum laden weight)	30 (48)	40 (64)	50 (80)	60 (96)

*The 30 mph limit usually applies to all traffic on all roads with street lighting unless signs show otherwise.
** 60 mph (96 km/h) if articulated or towing a trailer.

Speed limits

124 You **MUST NOT** exceed the maximum speed limits for the road and for your vehicle (see the table on page 37). The presence of street lights generally means that there is a 30 mph (48 km/h) speed limit unless otherwise specified.

Law RTRA sects 81, 86, 89 & sch 6

125 The speed limit is the absolute maximum and does not mean it is safe to drive at that speed irrespective of conditions. Driving at speeds too fast for the road and traffic conditions is dangerous. You should always reduce your speed when

- the road layout or condition presents hazards, such as bends
- sharing the road with pedestrians, cyclists and horse riders, particularly children, and motorcyclists
- weather conditions make it safer to do so
- driving at night as it is more difficult to see other road users.

126 **Stopping Distances.** Drive at a speed that will allow you to stop well within the distance you can see to be clear. You should

Typical Stopping Distances

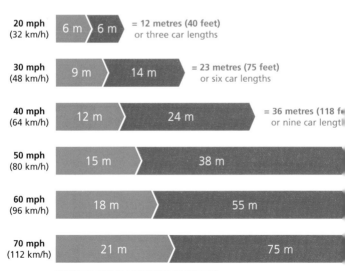

20 mph (32 km/h)	6 m · 6 m	= 12 metres (40 feet) or three car lengths
30 mph (48 km/h)	9 m · 14 m	= 23 metres (75 feet) or six car lengths
40 mph (64 km/h)	12 m · 24 m	= 36 metres (118 fe) or nine car lengt
50 mph (80 km/h)	15 m · 38 m	
60 mph (96 km/h)	18 m · 55 m	
70 mph (112 km/h)	21 m · 75 m	

The distances shown are a general guide. The distance will depend on your attention (thinking distance), the road surface, the weather conditions and the condition of your vehicle at the time.

Rule 126 – *Use a fixed point to help measure a two-second gap*

○ leave enough space between you and the vehicle
in front so that you can pull up safely if it suddenly
slows down or stops. The safe rule is never to get
closer than the overall stopping distance (see Typical
Stopping Distances diagram, shown below)

○ allow at least a two-second gap between you and
the vehicle in front on roads carrying faster-moving
traffic and in tunnels where visibility is reduced. The
gap should be at least doubled on wet roads and
increased still further on icy roads

○ remember, large vehicles and motorcycles need a
greater distance to stop. If driving a large vehicle
in a tunnel, you should allow a four-second gap
between you and the vehicle in front.

If you have to stop in a tunnel, leave at least a 5-metre
gap between you and the vehicle in front.

Thinking Distance	Braking Distance

Average car length = 4 metres (13 feet)

53 metres (175 feet)
or thirteen car lengths

= 73 metres (240 feet)
or eighteen car lengths

= 96 metres (315 feet)
or twenty-four car lengths

Lines and lane markings on the road

Diagrams of all lines are on pages 108–111.

127 **A broken white line.** This marks the centre of the road. When this line lengthens and the gaps shorten, it means that there is a hazard ahead. Do not cross it unless you can see the road is clear and wish to overtake or turn off.

128 **Double white lines where the line nearest to you is broken.** This means you may cross the lines to overtake if it is safe, provided you can complete the manoeuvre before reaching a solid white line on your side. White direction arrows on the road indicate that you need to get back onto your side of the road.

129 **Double white lines where the line nearest you is solid.** This means you **MUST NOT** cross or straddle it unless it is safe and you need to enter adjoining premises or a side road. You may cross the line if necessary, provided the road is clear, to pass a stationary vehicle, or overtake a pedal cycle, horse or road maintenance vehicle, if they are travelling at 10 mph (16 km/h) or less.

Laws RTA 1988 sect 36 & TSRGD regs 10 & 26

130 **Areas of white diagonal stripes** or chevrons painted on the road. These are to separate traffic lanes or to protect traffic turning right.

- ↻ If the area is bordered by a broken white line, you should not enter the area unless it is necessary and you can see that it is safe to do so.
- ↻ If the area is marked with chevrons and bordered by solid white lines you **MUST NOT** enter it except in an emergency.

Laws MT(E&W)R regs 5, 9, 10 & 16, MT(S)R regs 4, 8, 9 & 14, RTA sect 36 & TSRGD 10(1)

131 **Lane dividers.** These are short, broken white lines which are used on wide carriageways to divide them into lanes. You should keep between them.

Rule 132 *– Reflective road studs mark the lanes
and edges of the carriageway*

132 **Reflective road studs** may be used with
white lines.

- White studs mark the lanes or the middle
  of the road.
- Red studs mark the left edge of the road.
- Amber studs mark the central reservation
  of a dual carriageway or motorway.
- Green studs mark the edge of the main
  carriageway at lay-bys and slip roads.
- Green/yellow studs indicate temporary
  adjustments to lane layouts, e.g. where
  road works are taking place.

Multi-lane carriageways

133 ### Lane discipline
If you need to change lane, first use your mirrors
and if necessary take a quick sideways glance to
make sure you will not force another road user
to change course or speed. When it is safe to
do so, signal to indicate your intentions to other
road users and when clear, move over.

134 You should follow the signs and road
markings and get into the lane as directed. In
congested road conditions do not change lanes
unnecessarily. Merging in turn is recommended
but only if safe and appropriate when vehicles
are travelling at a very low speed, e.g. when
approaching road works or a road traffic
incident. It is not recommended at high speed.

Single carriageway

135 Where a single carriageway has three lanes and the road markings or signs do not give priority to traffic in either direction

- ↪ use the middle lane only for overtaking or turning right. Remember, you have no more right to use the middle lane than a driver coming from the opposite direction
- ↪ do not use the right-hand lane.

136 Where a single carriageway has four or more lanes, use only the lanes that signs or markings indicate.

Dual carriageways

A dual carriageway is a road which has a central reservation to separate the carriageways.

137 On a two-lane dual carriageway you should stay in the left-hand lane. Use the right-hand lane for overtaking or turning right. After overtaking, move back to the left-hand lane when it is safe to do so.

138 On a three-lane dual carriageway, you may use the middle lane or the right-hand lane to overtake but return to the middle and then the left-hand lane when it is safe.

139 **Climbing and crawler lanes.** These are provided on some hills. Use this lane if you are driving a slow-moving vehicle or if there are vehicles behind you wishing to overtake. Be aware of the signs and road markings which indicate the lane is about to end.

140 **Cycle lanes.** These are shown by road markings and signs. You **MUST NOT** drive or park in a cycle lane marked by a solid white line during its times of operation. Do not drive or park in a cycle lane marked by a broken white line unless it is unavoidable. You **MUST NOT** park in any cycle lane whilst waiting restrictions apply.

Law RTRA sects 5 & 8

141 **Bus lanes.** These are shown by road markings and signs that indicate which (if any) other vehicles are permitted to use the bus lane. Unless otherwise indicated, you should not drive in a bus lane during its period of operation. You may enter a bus lane to stop, to load or unload where this is not prohibited.

142 **High-occupancy vehicle lanes and other designated vehicle lanes.** Lanes may be restricted for use by particular types of vehicle; these restrictions may apply some or all of the time. The operating times and vehicle types will be indicated on the accompanying traffic signs. You **MUST NOT** drive in such lanes during their times of operation unless signs indicate that your vehicle is permitted (see page 106).

Vehicles permitted to use designated lanes may or may not include cycles, buses, taxis, licensed private hire vehicles, motorcycles, heavy goods vehicles (HGVs) and high-occupancy vehicles (HOVs).

Where HOV lanes are in operation, they **MUST ONLY** be used by

 vehicles containing at least the minimum number of people indicated on the traffic signs
 any other vehicles, such as buses and motorcycles, as indicated on signs prior to the start of the lane, irrespective of the number of occupants.

Laws RTRA sects 5 & 8, & RTA 1988, sect 36

143 **One-way streets.** Traffic **MUST** travel in the direction indicated by signs. Buses and/or cycles may have a contraflow lane. Choose the correct lane for your exit as soon as you can. Do not change lanes suddenly. Unless road signs or markings indicate otherwise, you should use

 the left-hand lane when going left
 the right-hand lane when going right
 the most appropriate lane when going straight ahead. Remember – traffic could be passing on both sides.

Laws RTA 1988 sect 36 & RTRA sects 5 & 8

General advice

144 **You MUST NOT**
 drive dangerously
 drive without due care and attention
 drive without reasonable consideration for other road users.

Law RTA 1988 sects 2 & 3 as amended by RTA 1991

145 You **MUST NOT** drive on or over a pavement, footpath or bridleway except to gain lawful access to property, or in the case of an emergency.
Laws HA 1835 sect 72 & RTA 1988 sect 34

146 **Adapt your driving** to the appropriate type and condition of road you are on. In particular

- do not treat speed limits as a target. It is often not appropriate or safe to drive at the maximum speed limit
- take the road and traffic conditions into account. Be prepared for unexpected or difficult situations, for example, the road being blocked beyond a blind bend. Be prepared to adjust your speed as a precaution
- where there are junctions, be prepared for road users emerging
- in side roads and country lanes look out for unmarked junctions where nobody has priority
- be prepared to stop at traffic control systems, road works, pedestrian crossings or traffic lights as necessary
- try to anticipate what pedestrians and cyclists might do. If pedestrians, particularly children, are looking the other way, they may step out into the road without seeing you.

147 **Be considerate.** Be careful of and considerate towards all types of road users, especially those requiring extra care (see Rule 204). You should

- try to be understanding if other road users cause problems; they may be inexperienced or not know the area well
- be patient; remember that anyone can make a mistake
- not allow yourself to become agitated or involved if someone is behaving badly on the road. This will only make the situation worse. Pull over, calm down and, when you feel relaxed, continue your journey
- slow down and hold back if a road user pulls out into your path at a junction. Allow them to get clear. Do not over-react by driving too close behind to intimidate them
- do not throw anything out of a vehicle, for example, cigarette ends, cans, paper or carrier bags. This can endanger other road users, particularly motorcyclists and cyclists.

148 ## Safe driving and riding needs concentration.
Avoid distractions when driving or riding such as

- loud music (this may mask other sounds)
- trying to read maps
- inserting a cassette or CD or tuning a radio
- arguing with your passengers or other
  road users
- eating and drinking
- smoking

You **MUST NOT** smoke in public transport
vehicles or in vehicles used for work purposes
in certain prescribed circumstances. Separate
regulations apply to England, Wales and Scotland.
Laws TSf(EV) regs 2007, TSfP(W) regs 2007 & TPSCP(S) regs 2006

Mobile phones and in-vehicle technology

149 You **MUST** exercise proper control of your vehicle
at all times. You **MUST NOT** use a hand-held
mobile phone, or similar device, when driving or
when supervising a learner driver, except to call
999 or 112 in a genuine emergency when it is
unsafe or impractical to stop. Never use a hand-
held microphone when driving. Using hands-free
equipment is also likely to distract your attention
from the road. It is far safer not to use any
telephone while you are driving or riding – find a
safe place to stop first or use the voicemail facility
and listen to messages later.
Laws RTA 1988 sects 2 & 3 & CUR regs 104 & 110

150 There is a danger of driver distraction being
caused by in-vehicle systems such as satellite
navigation systems, congestion warning systems,
PCs, multi-media, etc. You **MUST** exercise
proper control of your vehicle at all times. Do
not rely on driver assistance systems such as
cruise control or lane departure warnings. They
are available to assist but you should not reduce
your concentration levels. Do not be distracted
by maps or screen-based information (such as
navigation or vehicle management systems)
while driving or riding. If necessary find
a safe place to stop.
Laws RTA 1988 sects 2 & 3 & CUR reg 104

Rule 151 – *Do not block access to a side road*

 In slow-moving traffic. You should

- reduce the distance between you and the vehicle ahead to maintain traffic flow
- never get so close to the vehicle in front that you cannot stop safely
- leave enough space to be able to manoeuvre if the vehicle in front breaks down or an emergency vehicle needs to get past
- not change lanes to the left to overtake
- allow access into and from side roads, as blocking these will add to congestion
- be aware of cyclists and motorcyclists who may be passing on either side.

 Driving in built-up areas

Residential streets. You should drive slowly and carefully on streets where there are likely to be pedestrians, cyclists and parked cars. In some areas a 20 mph (32 km/h) maximum speed limit may be in force. Look out for

- vehicles emerging from junctions or driveways
- vehicles moving off
- car doors opening
- pedestrians
- children running out from between parked cars
- cyclists and motorcyclists.

Rule 153 – *Chicanes may be used to slow traffic down*

153 **Traffic-calming measures.** On some roads there are features such as road humps, chicanes and narrowings which are intended to slow you down. When you approach these features reduce your speed. Allow cyclists and motorcyclists room to pass through them. Maintain a reduced speed along the whole of the stretch of road within the calming measures. Give way to oncoming road users if directed to do so by signs. You should not overtake other moving road users while in these areas.

Country roads

154 Take extra care on country roads and reduce your speed at approaches to bends, which can be sharper than they appear, and at junctions and turnings, which may be partially hidden. Be prepared for pedestrians, horse riders, cyclists, slow-moving farm vehicles or mud on the road surface. Make sure you can stop within the distance you can see to be clear. You should also reduce your speed where country roads enter villages.

155 **Single-track roads.** These are only wide enough for one vehicle. They may have special passing places. If you see a vehicle coming towards you, or the driver behind wants to overtake, pull into a passing place on your left, or wait opposite a passing place on your right. Give way to vehicles coming uphill whenever you can. If necessary, reverse until you reach a passing place to let the other vehicle pass. Slow down when passing pedestrians, cyclists and horse riders.

156 Do not park in passing places.

Vehicles prohibited from using roads and pavements

157 Certain motorised vehicles do not meet the construction and technical requirements for road vehicles and are generally not intended, not suitable and not legal for road, pavement, footpath, cycle path or bridleway use. These include most types of miniature motorcycles, also called mini motos, and motorised scooters, also called go peds, which are powered by electric or internal combustion engines. These types of vehicle **MUST NOT** be used on roads, pavements, footpaths or bridleways.

Laws RTA 1988 sects 34, 41a, 42, 47, 63 & 66, HA 1835, sect 72, & R(S)A sect 129

158 Certain models of motorcycles, motor tricycles and quadricycles, also called quad bikes, are suitable only for off-road use and do not meet legal standards for use on roads. Vehicles that do not meet these standards **MUST NOT** be used on roads. They **MUST NOT** be used on pavements, footpaths, cycle paths or bridleways either. You **MUST** make sure that any motorcycle, motor tricycle, quadricycle or any other motor vehicle meets legal standards and is properly registered, taxed and insured before using it on the roads. Even when registered, taxed and insured for the road, vehicles **MUST NOT** be used on pavements.

Laws RTA 1988 sects 34, 41a, 42, 47, 63, 66 & 156, HA 1835, sect 72, R(S)A sect 129, & VERA sects 1, 29, 31A, & 43A

Using the Road

General rules

159 Before moving off you should

- ◯ use all mirrors to check the road is clear
- ◯ look round to check the blind spots (the areas you are unable to see in the mirrors)
- ◯ signal if necessary before moving out
- ◯ look round for a final check.

Move off only when it is safe to do so.

Rule 159 – Check the blind spot before moving off

160 **Once moving** you should

- ◯ keep to the left, unless road signs or markings indicate otherwise. The exceptions are when you want to overtake, turn right or pass parked vehicles or pedestrians in the road
- ◯ keep well to the left on right-hand bends. This will improve your view of the road and help avoid the risk of colliding with traffic approaching from the opposite direction
- ◯ drive with both hands on the wheel where possible. This will help you to remain in full control of the vehicle at all times

- be aware of other road users, especially cycles and motorcycles who may be filtering through the traffic. These are more difficult to see than larger vehicles and their riders are particularly vulnerable. Give them plenty of room, especially if you are driving a long vehicle or towing a trailer
- select a lower gear before you reach a long downhill slope. This will help to control your speed
- when towing, remember the extra length will affect overtaking and manoeuvring. The extra weight will also affect the braking and acceleration.

161 **Mirrors.** All mirrors should be used effectively throughout your journey. You should

- use your mirrors frequently so that you always know what is behind and to each side of you
- use them in good time before you signal or change direction or speed
- be aware that mirrors do not cover all areas and there will be blind spots. You will need to look round and check.

Remember: Mirrors – Signal – Manoeuvre

Overtaking

162 **Before overtaking** you should make sure

- the road is sufficiently clear ahead
- road users are not beginning to overtake you
- there is a suitable gap in front of the road user you plan to overtake.

163 **Overtake only** when it is safe and legal to do so. You should

- not get too close to the vehicle you intend to overtake
- use your mirrors, signal when it is safe to do so, take a quick sideways glance if necessary into the blind spot area and then start to move out
- not assume that you can simply follow a vehicle ahead which is overtaking; there may only be enough room for one vehicle

- move quickly past the vehicle you are overtaking, once you have started to overtake. Allow plenty of room. Move back to the left as soon as you can but do not cut in

- take extra care at night and in poor visibility when it is harder to judge speed and distance

- give way to oncoming vehicles before passing parked vehicles or other obstructions on your side of the road

- only overtake on the left if the vehicle in front is signalling to turn right, and there is room to do so

- stay in your lane if traffic is moving slowly in queues. If the queue on your right is moving more slowly than you are, you may pass on the left

- give motorcyclists, cyclists and horse riders at least as much room as you would when overtaking a car (see Rules 211–215).

Remember: Mirrors – Signal – Manoeuvre

Rule 163 – *Give vulnerable road users at least as much space as you would a car*

Large vehicles. Overtaking these is more difficult. You should

- drop back. This will increase your ability to see ahead and should allow the driver of the large vehicle to see you in their mirrors. Getting too close to large vehicles, including agricultural vehicles such as a tractor with a trailer or other fixed equipment, will obscure your view of the road ahead and there may be another slow-moving vehicle in front
- make sure that you have enough room to complete your overtaking manoeuvre before committing yourself. It takes longer to pass a large vehicle. If in doubt do not overtake
- not assume you can follow a vehicle ahead which is overtaking a long vehicle. If a problem develops, they may abort overtaking and pull back in.

Rule 164 – *Do not cut in too quickly*

You **MUST NOT** overtake

- if you would have to cross or straddle double white lines with a solid line nearest to you (but see Rule129)
- if you would have to enter an area designed to divide traffic, if it is surrounded by a solid white line
- the nearest vehicle to a pedestrian crossing, especially when it has stopped to let pedestrians cross
- if you would have to enter a lane reserved for buses, trams or cycles during its hours of operation
- after a 'No Overtaking' sign and until you pass a sign cancelling the restriction.

Laws RTA 1988 sect 36, TSRGD regs 10, 22, 23 & 24, ZPPPCRGD reg 24

166 **DO NOT** overtake if there is any doubt, or where you cannot see far enough ahead to be sure it is safe. For example, when you are approaching

- a corner or bend
- a hump bridge
- the brow of a hill.

167 **DO NOT** overtake where you might come into conflict with other road users. For example

- approaching or at a road junction on either side of the road
- where the road narrows
- when approaching a school crossing patrol
- between the kerb and a bus or tram when it is at a stop
- where traffic is queuing at junctions or road works
- when you would force another road user to swerve or slow down
- at a level crossing
- when a road user is indicating right, even if you believe the signal should have been cancelled. Do not take a risk; wait for the signal to be cancelled
- stay behind if you are following a cyclist approaching a roundabout or junction, and you intend to turn left
- when a tram is standing at a kerbside tram stop and there is no clearly marked passing lane for other traffic.

168 **Being overtaken.** If a driver is trying to overtake you, maintain a steady course and speed, slowing down if necessary to let the vehicle pass. Never obstruct drivers who wish to pass. Speeding up or driving unpredictably while someone is overtaking you is dangerous. Drop back to maintain a two-second gap if someone overtakes and pulls into the gap in front of you.

169 Do not hold up a long queue of traffic, especially if you are driving a large or slow-moving vehicle. Check your mirrors frequently, and if necessary, pull in where it is safe and let traffic pass.

Road junctions

170 Take extra care at junctions. You should

- ⊙ watch out for cyclists, motorcyclists, powered wheelchairs/mobility scooters and pedestrians as they are not always easy to see. Be aware that they may not have seen or heard you if you are approaching from behind
- ⊙ watch out for pedestrians crossing a road into which you are turning. If they have started to cross they have priority, so give way
- ⊙ watch out for long vehicles which may be turning at a junction ahead; they may have to use the whole width of the road to make the turn (see Rule 221)
- ⊙ watch out for horse riders who may take a different line on the road from that which you would expect
- ⊙ not assume, when waiting at a junction, that a vehicle coming from the right and signalling left will actually turn. Wait and make sure
- ⊙ look all around before emerging. Do not cross or join a road until there is a gap large enough for you to do so safely.

Rule 170 – *Give way to pedestrians who have started to cross*

171 You **MUST** stop behind the line at a junction with a 'Stop' sign and a solid white line across the road. Wait for a safe gap in the traffic before you move off.

Laws RTA 1988 sect 36 & TSRGD regs 10 & 16

172 The approach to a junction may have a 'Give Way' sign or a triangle marked on the road. You **MUST** give way to traffic on the main road when emerging from a junction with broken white lines across the road.

Laws RTA 1988 sect 36 & TSRGD regs 10(1),16(1) & 25

Rule 173 – *Assess your vehicle's length and do not obstruct traffic*

173 **Dual carriageways.** When crossing or turning right, first assess whether the central reservation is deep enough to protect the full length of your vehicle.

- If it is, then you should treat each half of the carriageway as a separate road. Wait in the central reservation until there is a safe gap in the traffic on the second half of the road.
- If the central reservation is too shallow for the length of your vehicle, wait until you can cross both carriageways in one go.

174 **Box junctions.** These have criss-cross yellow lines painted on the road (see page 110). You **MUST NOT** enter the box until your exit road or lane is clear. However, you may enter the box and wait when you want to turn right, and are only stopped from doing so by oncoming traffic, or by other vehicles waiting to turn right. At signalled roundabouts you **MUST NOT** enter the box unless you can cross over it completely without stopping. Law TSRGD regs 10(1) & 29(2)

Rule 174 – *Enter a box junction only if your exit road is clear*

Junctions controlled by traffic lights

175 You **MUST** stop behind the white 'Stop' line across your side of the road unless the light is green. If the amber light appears you may go on only if you have already crossed the stop line or are so close to it that to stop might cause a collision.

Laws RTA 1988 sect 36 & TSRGD regs 10 & 36

176 You **MUST NOT** move forward over the white line when the red light is showing. Only go forward when the traffic lights are green if there is room for you to clear the junction safely or you are taking up a position to turn right. If the traffic lights are not working, treat the situation as you would an unmarked junction and proceed with great care.

Laws RTA 1988 sect 36 & TSRGD regs 10 & 36

177 **Green filter arrow.** This indicates a filter lane only. Do not enter that lane unless you want to go in the direction of the arrow. You may proceed in the direction of the green arrow when it, or the full green light shows. Give other traffic, especially cyclists, time and room to move into the correct lane.

178 **Advanced stop lines.** Some signal-controlled junctions have advanced stop lines to allow cycles to be positioned ahead of other traffic. Motorists, including motorcyclists, **MUST** stop at the first white line reached if the lights are amber or red and should avoid blocking the way or encroaching on the marked area at other times, e.g. if the junction ahead is blocked. If your vehicle has proceeded over the first white line at the time that the signal goes red, you **MUST** stop at the second white line, even if your vehicle is in the marked area. Allow cyclists time and space to move off when the green signal shows.

Laws RTA 1988 sect 36 & TSRGD regs 10, 36(1) & 43(2)

Rule 178 – Do not encroach on the cyclists' waiting area

Turning right

179 **Well before** you turn right you should

○ use your mirrors to make sure you know the position and movement of traffic behind you
○ give a right-turn signal
○ take up a position just left of the middle of the road or in the space marked for traffic turning right
○ leave room for other vehicles to pass on the left, if possible.

180 Wait until there is a safe gap between you and any oncoming vehicle. Watch out for cyclists, motorcyclists, pedestrians and other road users. Check your mirrors and blind spot again to make sure you are not being overtaken, then make the turn. Do not cut the corner. Take great care when turning into a main road; you will need to watch for traffic in both directions and wait for a safe gap.

Remember: Mirrors – Signal – Manoeuvre

Rule 180 – Position your vehicle correctly to avoid obstructing traffic

181 **When turning** right at crossroads where an oncoming vehicle is also turning right, there is a choice of two methods

○ turn right side to right side; keep the other vehicle on your right and turn behind it. This is generally the safer method as you have a clear view of any approaching traffic when completing your turn

○ left side to left side, turning in front of each other. This can block your view of oncoming vehicles, so take extra care. Cyclists and motorcyclists in particular may be hidden from your view. Road layout, markings or how the other vehicle is positioned can determine which course should be taken.

Rule 181 – Left – Turning right side to right side. Right – Turning left side to left side.

Turning left

182 Use your mirrors and give a left-turn signal well before you turn left. Do not overtake just before you turn left and watch out for traffic coming up on your left before you make the turn, especially if driving a large vehicle. Cyclists, motorcyclists and other road users in particular may be hidden from your view.

Rule 182 – Do not cut in on cyclists

183 When turning

○ keep as close to the left as is safe and practicable
○ give way to any vehicles using a bus lane, cycle lane or tramway from either direction.

Roundabouts

 184 **On approaching a roundabout** take notice and act on all the information available to you, including traffic signs, traffic lights and lane markings which direct you into the correct lane. You should

- ⊃ use **Mirrors – Signal – Manoeuvre** at all stages
- ⊃ decide as early as possible which exit you need to take
- ⊃ give an appropriate signal (see Rule 186). Time your signals so as not to confuse other road users
- ⊃ get into the correct lane
- ⊃ adjust your speed and position to fit in with traffic conditions
- ⊃ be aware of the speed and position of all the road users around you.

185 **When reaching the roundabout** you should

- ⊃ give priority to traffic approaching from your right, unless directed otherwise by signs, road markings or traffic lights
- ⊃ check whether road markings allow you to enter the roundabout without giving way. If so, proceed, but still look to the right before joining
- ⊃ watch out for all other road users already on the roundabout; be aware they may not be signalling correctly or at all
- ⊃ look forward before moving off to make sure traffic in front has moved off.

Rule 185 – *Follow the correct procedure at roundabouts*

186 **Signals and position.** When taking the first exit, unless signs or markings indicate otherwise

- signal left and approach in the left-hand lane
- keep to the left on the roundabout and continue signalling left to leave.

When taking an exit to the right or going full circle, unless signs or markings indicate otherwise

- signal right and approach in the right-hand lane
- keep to the right on the roundabout until you need to change lanes to exit the roundabout
- signal left after you have passed the exit before the one you want.

When taking any intermediate exit, unless signs or markings indicate otherwise

- select the appropriate lane on approach to and on the roundabout
- you should not normally need to signal on approach
- stay in this lane until you need to alter course to exit the roundabout
- signal left after you have passed the exit before the one you want.

When there are more than three lanes at the entrance to a roundabout, use the most appropriate lane on approach and through it.

187 **In all cases watch out for** and give plenty of room to

- pedestrians who may be crossing the approach and exit roads
- traffic crossing in front of you on the roundabout, especially vehicles intending to leave by the next exit
- traffic which may be straddling lanes or positioned incorrectly
- motorcyclists
- cyclists and horse riders who may stay in the left-hand lane and signal right if they intend to continue round the roundabout. Allow them to do so
- long vehicles (including those towing trailers). These might have to take a different course or straddle lanes either approaching or on the roundabout because of their length. Watch out for their signals.

188 **Mini-roundabouts.** Approach these in the same way as normal roundabouts. All vehicles **MUST** pass round the central markings except large vehicles which are physically incapable of doing so. Remember, there is less space to manoeuvre and less time to signal. Avoid making U-turns at mini-roundabouts. Beware of others doing this.
Laws RTA 1988 sect 36 & TSRGD regs 10(1) & 16(1)

189 At double mini-roundabouts treat each roundabout separately and give way to traffic from the right.

190 **Multiple roundabouts.** At some complex junctions, there may be a series of mini-roundabouts at each intersection. Treat each mini-roundabout separately and follow the normal rules.

Rule 190 *– Treat each roundabout separately*

Pedestrian crossings

191 You **MUST NOT** park on a crossing or in the area covered by the zig-zag lines. You **MUST NOT** overtake the moving vehicle nearest the crossing or the vehicle nearest the crossing which has stopped to give way to pedestrians.
Laws ZPPPCRGD regs 18, 20 & 24, RTRA sect 25(5) & TSRGD regs 10, 27 & 28

192 In queuing traffic, you should keep the crossing clear.

Rule 192 – *Keep the crossing clear*

193 You should take extra care where the view of either side of the crossing is blocked by queuing traffic or incorrectly parked vehicles. Pedestrians may be crossing between stationary vehicles.

194 Allow pedestrians plenty of time to cross and do not harass them by revving your engine or edging forward.

195 **Zebra crossings.** As you approach a zebra crossing

- ⊙ look out for pedestrians waiting to cross and be ready to slow down or stop to let them cross
- ⊙ you **MUST** give way when a pedestrian has moved onto a crossing
- ⊙ allow more time for stopping on wet or icy roads
- ⊙ do not wave or use your horn to invite pedestrians across; this could be dangerous if another vehicle is approaching
- ⊙ be aware of pedestrians approaching from the side of the crossing.

A zebra crossing with a central island is two separate crossings (see pictures on page 10).
Law ZPPPCRGD reg 25

196 Signal-controlled crossings

Pelican crossings. These are signal-controlled crossings where flashing amber follows the red 'Stop' light. You **MUST** stop when the red light shows. When the amber light is flashing, you **MUST** give way to any pedestrians on the crossing. If the amber light is flashing and there are no pedestrians on the crossing, you may proceed with caution.

Laws ZPPPCRGD regs 23 & 26 & RTRA sect 25(5)

Rule 196 – Allow pedestrians to cross when the amber light is flashing

197

Pelican crossings which go straight across the road are one crossing, even when there is a central island. You **MUST** wait for pedestrians who are crossing from the other side of the island.

Laws ZPPPCRGD reg 26 & RTRA sect 25(5)

198

Give way to anyone still crossing after the signal for vehicles has changed to green. This advice applies to all crossings.

199

Toucan, puffin and equestrian crossings. These are similar to pelican crossings, but there is no flashing amber phase; the light sequence for traffic at these three crossings is the same as at traffic lights. If the signal-controlled crossing is not working, proceed with extreme caution.

Reversing

200 Choose an appropriate place to manoeuvre. If you need to turn your vehicle around, wait until you find a safe place. Try not to reverse or turn round in a busy road; find a quiet side road or drive round a block of side streets.

201 Do not reverse from a side road into a main road. When using a driveway, reverse in and drive out if you can.

202 Look carefully before you start reversing. You should

- ↻ use all your mirrors
- ↻ check the 'blind spot' behind you (the part of the road you cannot see easily in the mirrors)
- ↻ check there are no pedestrians (particularly children), cyclists, other road users or obstructions in the road behind you.

Rule 202 *– Check all round when reversing*

Reverse slowly while

- ↻ checking all around
- ↻ looking mainly through the rear window
- ↻ being aware that the front of your vehicle will swing out as you turn.

Get someone to guide you if you cannot see clearly.

203 You **MUST NOT** reverse your vehicle further than necessary.
Law CUR reg 106

Road users requiring extra care

204 The most vulnerable road users are pedestrians, cyclists, motorcyclists and horse riders. It is particularly important to be aware of children, older and disabled people, and learner and inexperienced drivers and riders.

Pedestrians

205 There is a risk of pedestrians, especially children, stepping unexpectedly into the road. You should drive with the safety of children in mind at a speed suitable for the conditions.

206 **Drive carefully and slowly** when

- in crowded shopping streets, Home Zones and Quiet Lanes (see Rule 218) or residential areas
- driving past bus and tram stops; pedestrians may emerge suddenly into the road
- passing parked vehicles, especially ice cream vans; children are more interested in ice cream than traffic and may run into the road unexpectedly
- needing to cross a pavement or cycle track; for example, to reach or leave a driveway. Give way to pedestrians and cyclists on the pavement
- reversing into a side road; look all around the vehicle and give way to any pedestrians who may be crossing the road
- turning at road junctions; give way to pedestrians who are already crossing the road into which you are turning
- the pavement is closed due to street repairs and pedestrians are directed to use the road
- approaching pedestrians on narrow rural roads without a footway or footpath. Always slow down and be prepared to stop if necessary, giving them plenty of room as you drive past.

Rule 206 – *Watch out for children in busy areas*

207 **Particularly vulnerable pedestrians.** These include

- ○ children and older pedestrians who may not be able to judge your speed and could step into the road in front of you. At 40 mph (64 km/h) your vehicle will probably kill any pedestrians it hits. At 20 mph (32 km/h) there is only a 1 in 20 chance of the pedestrian being killed. So kill your speed
- ○ older pedestrians who may need more time to cross the road. Be patient and allow them to cross in their own time. Do not hurry them by revving your engine or edging forward
- ○ people with disabilities. People with hearing impairments may not be aware of your vehicle approaching. Those with walking difficulties require more time
- ○ blind or partially sighted people, who may be carrying a white cane using a guide dog. They may not be able to see you approaching
- ○ deafblind people who may be carrying a white cane with a red band or using a dog with a red and white harness. They may not see or hear instructions or signals.

208 **Near schools.** Drive slowly and be particularly aware of young cyclists and pedestrians. In some places, there may be a flashing amber signal below the 'School' warning sign which tells you that there may be children crossing the road ahead. Drive very slowly until you are clear of the area.

209 Drive carefully and slowly when passing a stationary bus showing a 'School Bus' sign (see page 111) as children may be getting on or off.

210 You **MUST** stop when a school crossing patrol shows a 'Stop for children' sign (see pages 98 & 100).

Law RTRA sect 28

Motorcyclists and cyclists

211 It is often difficult to see motorcyclists and cyclists, especially when they are coming up from behind, coming out of junctions, at roundabouts, overtaking you or filtering through traffic. Always look out for them before you emerge from a junction; they could be approaching faster than you think. When turning right across a line of slow-moving or stationary traffic, look out for cyclists or motorcyclists on the inside of the traffic you are crossing. Be especially careful when turning, and when changing direction or lane. Be sure to check mirrors and blind spots carefully.

Rule 211 *– Look out for motorcyclists and cyclists at junctions*

212 When passing motorcyclists and cyclists, give them plenty of room (see Rules 162–167). If they look over their shoulder it could mean that they intend to pull out, turn right or change direction. Give them time and space to do so.

213 Motorcyclists and cyclists may suddenly need to avoid uneven road surfaces and obstacles such as drain covers or oily, wet or icy patches on the road. Give them plenty of room and pay particular attention to any sudden change of direction they may have to make.

67

Other road users

214 **Animals.** When passing animals, drive slowly. Give them plenty of room and be ready to stop. Do not scare animals by sounding your horn, revving your engine or accelerating rapidly once you have passed them. Look out for animals being led, driven or ridden on the road and take extra care. Keep your speed down at bends and on narrow country roads. If a road is blocked by a herd of animals, stop and switch off your engine until they have left the road. Watch out for animals on unfenced roads.

215 **Horse riders and horse-drawn vehicles.** Be particularly careful of horse riders and horse-drawn vehicles especially when overtaking. Always pass wide and slowly. Horse riders are often children, so take extra care and remember riders may ride in double file when escorting a young or inexperienced horse or rider. Look out for horse riders' and horse drivers' signals and heed a request to slow down or stop. Take great care and treat all horses as a potential hazard; they can be unpredictable, despite the efforts of their rider/driver.

216 **Older drivers.** Their reactions may be slower than other drivers. Make allowance for this.

217 **Learners and inexperienced drivers.** They may not be so skilful at anticipating and responding to events. Be particularly patient with learner drivers and young drivers. Drivers who have recently passed their test may display a 'new driver' plate or sticker (see Annex 8 – Safety code for new drivers).

218 **Home Zones and Quiet Lanes.** These are places where people could be using the whole of the road for a range of activities such as children playing or for a community event. You should drive slowly and carefully and be prepared to stop to allow people extra time to make space for you to pass them in safety.

Other vehicles

219 **Emergency and Incident Support vehicles.** You should look and listen for ambulances, fire engines, police, doctors or other emergency vehicles using flashing blue, red or green lights and sirens or flashing headlights, or Highways Agency Traffic Officer and Incident Support vehicles using flashing amber lights. When one approaches do not panic. Consider the route of such a vehicle and take appropriate action to let it pass, while complying with all traffic signs. If necessary, pull to the side of the road and stop, but try to avoid stopping before the brow of a hill, a bend or narrow section of road. Do not endanger yourself, other road users or pedestrians and avoid mounting the kerb. Do not brake harshly on approach to a junction or roundabout, as a following vehicle may not have the same view as you.

220 **Powered vehicles used by disabled people.** These small vehicles travel at a maximum speed of 8 mph (12 km/h). On a dual carriageway where the speed limit exceeds 50 mph (80 km/h) they **MUST** have a flashing amber beacon, but on other roads you may not have that advance warning (see Rules 36–46 inclusive).

Law RVLR reg 17(1) & 26

221 **Large vehicles.** These may need extra road space to turn or to deal with a hazard that you are not able to see. If you are following a large vehicle, such as a bus or articulated lorry, be aware that the driver may not be able to see you in the mirrors. Be prepared to stop and wait if it needs room or time to turn.

Rule 221 – Large vehicles need extra room

222 Large vehicles can block your view. Your ability to see and to plan ahead will be improved if you pull back to increase your separation distance. Be patient, as larger vehicles are subject to lower speed limits than cars and motorcycles. Many large vehicles may be fitted with speed limiting devices which will restrict speed to 56 mph (90 km/h) even on a motorway.

223 **Buses, coaches and trams.** Give priority to these vehicles when you can do so safely, especially when they signal to pull away from stops. Look out for people getting off a bus or tram and crossing the road.

224 **Electric vehicles.** Be careful of electric vehicles such as milk floats and trams. Trams move quickly but silently and cannot steer to avoid you.

225 **Vehicles with flashing amber beacons.** These warn of a slow-moving or stationary vehicle (such as a Traffic Officer vehicle, salt spreader, snow plough or recovery vehicle) or abnormal loads, so approach with caution. On unrestricted dual carriageways, motor vehicles first used on or after 1 January 1947 with a maximum speed of 25 mph (40 km/h) or less (such as tractors) **MUST** use a flashing amber beacon (also see Rule 220).

Law RVLR 1989, reg 17

Driving in adverse weather conditions

226 You **MUST** use headlights when visibility is seriously reduced, generally when you cannot see for more than 100 metres (328 feet). You may also use front or rear fog lights but you **MUST** switch them off when visibility improves (see Rule 236).

Law RVLR regs 25 & 27

227 **Wet weather.** In wet weather, stopping distances will be at least double those required for stopping on dry roads (see pages 38–39). This is because your tyres have less grip on the road. In wet weather

- ⊃ you should keep well back from the vehicle in front. This will increase your ability to see and plan ahead
- ⊃ if the steering becomes unresponsive, it probably means that water is preventing the tyres from gripping the road. Ease off the accelerator and slow down gradually
- ⊃ the rain and spray from vehicles may make it difficult to see and be seen
- ⊃ be aware of the dangers of spilt diesel that will make the surface very slippery (see Annex 6)
- ⊃ take extra care around pedestrians, cyclists, motorcyclists and horse riders.

Icy and snowy weather

228 In winter check the local weather forecast for warnings of icy or snowy weather. **DO NOT** drive in these conditions unless your journey is essential. If it is, take great care and allow more time for your journey. Take an emergency kit of de-icer and ice scraper, torch, warm clothing and boots, first aid kit, jump leads and a shovel, together with a warm drink and emergency food in case you get stuck or your vehicle breaks down.

Before you set off

- you **MUST** be able to see, so clear all snow and ice from all your windows
- you **MUST** ensure that lights are clean and number plates are clearly visible and legible
- make sure the mirrors are clear and the windows are demisted thoroughly
- remove all snow that might fall off into the path of other road users
- check your planned route is clear of delays and that no further snowfalls or severe weather are predicted.

Laws CUR reg 30, RVLR reg 23, VERA sect 43 & RV(DRM)R reg 11

Rule 229 – Make sure your windscreen is completely clear

230 **When driving** in icy or snowy weather

- ⊘ drive with care, even if the roads have been treated
- ⊘ keep well back from the road user in front as stopping distances can be ten times greater than on dry roads
- ⊘ take care when overtaking vehicles spreading salt or other de-icer, particularly if you are riding a motorcycle or cycle
- ⊘ watch out for snowploughs which may throw out snow on either side. Do not overtake them unless the lane you intend to use has been cleared
- ⊘ be prepared for the road conditions to change over relatively short distances
- ⊘ listen to travel bulletins and take note of variable message signs that may provide information about weather, road and traffic conditions ahead.

231 **Drive extremely carefully** when the roads are icy. Avoid sudden actions as these could cause loss of control. You should

- ⊘ drive at a slow speed in as high a gear as possible; accelerate and brake very gently
- ⊘ drive particularly slowly on bends where loss of control is more likely. Brake progressively on the straight before you reach a bend. Having slowed down, steer smoothly round the bend, avoiding sudden actions
- ⊘ check your grip on the road surface when there is snow or ice by choosing a safe place to brake gently. If the steering feels unresponsive this may indicate ice and your vehicle losing its grip on the road. When travelling on ice, tyres make virtually no noise.

Windy weather

232 High-sided vehicles are most affected by windy weather, but strong gusts can also blow a car, cyclist, motorcyclist or horse rider off course. This can happen on open stretches of road exposed to strong crosswinds, or when passing bridges or gaps in hedges.

233 In very windy weather your vehicle may be affected by turbulence created by large vehicles. Motorcyclists are particularly affected, so keep well back from them when they are overtaking a high-sided vehicle.

Fog

234 **Before entering fog** check your mirrors then slow down. If the word 'Fog' is shown on a roadside signal but the road is clear, be prepared for a bank of fog or drifting patchy fog ahead. Even if it seems to be clearing, you can suddenly find yourself in thick fog.

235 **When driving in fog** you should

- use your lights as required (see Rule 226)
- keep a safe distance behind the vehicle in front. Rear lights can give a false sense of security
- be able to pull up well within the distance you can see clearly. This is particularly important on motorways and dual carriageways, as vehicles are travelling faster
- use your windscreen wipers and demisters
- beware of other drivers not using headlights
- not accelerate to get away from a vehicle which is too close behind you
- check your mirrors before you slow down. Then use your brakes so that your brake lights warn drivers behind you that you are slowing down
- stop in the correct position at a junction with limited visibility and listen for traffic. When you are sure it is safe to emerge, do so positively and do not hesitate in a position that puts you directly in the path of approaching vehicles.

236 You **MUST NOT** use front or rear fog lights unless visibility is seriously reduced (see Rule 226) as they dazzle other road users and can obscure your brake lights. You **MUST** switch them off when visibility improves.

Law RVLR regs 25 & 27

237 **Hot weather.** Keep your vehicle well ventilated to avoid drowsiness. Be aware that the road surface may become soft or if it rains after a dry spell it may become slippery. These conditions could affect your steering and braking. If you are dazzled by bright sunlight, slow down and if necessary, stop.

Waiting and parking

238 You **MUST NOT** wait or park on yellow lines during the times of operation shown on nearby time plates (or zone entry signs if in a Controlled Parking Zone) – see pages 106 and 109. Double yellow lines indicate a prohibition of waiting at any time even if there are no upright signs. You **MUST NOT** wait or park, or stop to set down and pick up passengers, on school entrance markings (see page 110) when upright signs indicate a prohibition of stopping.

Law RTRA sects 5 & 8

Parking

239 Use off-street parking areas, or bays marked out with white lines on the road as parking places, wherever possible. If you have to stop on the roadside

- ↻ do not park facing against the traffic flow
- ↻ stop as close as you can to the side
- ↻ do not stop too close to a vehicle displaying a Blue Badge: remember, the occupant may need more room to get in or out
- ↻ you **MUST** switch off the engine, headlights and fog lights
- ↻ you **MUST** apply the handbrake before leaving the vehicle

Rule 239 – Check before opening your door

- you **MUST** ensure you do not hit anyone when you open your door. Check for cyclists or other traffic
- it is safer for your passengers (especially children) to get out of the vehicle on the side next to the kerb
- put all valuables out of sight and make sure your vehicle is secure
- lock your vehicle.

Laws CUR reg 98, 105 & 107, RVLR reg 27 & RTA 1988 sect 42

240 You **MUST NOT** stop or park on

- the carriageway or the hard shoulder of a motorway except in an emergency (see Rule 270)
- a pedestrian crossing, including the area marked by the zig-zag lines (see Rule 191)
- a clearway (see page 101)
- taxi bays as indicated by upright signs and markings
- an Urban Clearway within its hours of operation, except to pick up or set down passengers (see page 101)
- a road marked with double white lines, even when a broken white line is on your side of the road, except to pick up or set down passengers, or to load or unload goods
- a tram or cycle lane during its period of operation
- a cycle track
- red lines, in the case of specially designated 'red routes', unless otherwise indicated by signs.

Any vehicle may enter a bus lane to stop, load or unload where this is not prohibited (see Rule 141).

Laws MT(E&W)R regs 7 & 9, MT(S)R regs 6 & 8, ZPPPCRGD regs 18 & 20, RTRA sects 5, 6 & 8, TSRGD regs 10, 26 & 27, RTA 1988 sects 21(1) & 36

241 You **MUST NOT** park in parking spaces reserved for specific users, such as Blue Badge holders, residents or motorcycles, unless entitled to do so.

Laws CSDPA sect 21 & RTRA sects 5 & 8

242 You **MUST NOT** leave your vehicle or trailer in a dangerous position or where it causes any unnecessary obstruction of the road.

Laws RTA 1988, sect 22 & CUR reg 103

243 **DO NOT** stop or park

- near a school entrance
- anywhere you would prevent access for Emergency Services
- at or near a bus or tram stop or taxi rank
- on the approach to a level crossing/tramway crossing
- opposite or within 10 metres (32 feet) of a junction, except in an authorised parking space
- near the brow of a hill or hump bridge
- opposite a traffic island or (if this would cause an obstruction) another parked vehicle
- where you would force other traffic to enter a tram lane
- where the kerb has been lowered to help wheelchair users and powered mobility vehicles
- in front of an entrance to a property
- on a bend
- where you would obstruct cyclists' use of cycle facilities *except* when forced to do so by stationary traffic.

244 You **MUST NOT** park partially or wholly on the pavement in London, and should not do so elsewhere unless signs permit it. Parking on the pavement can obstruct and seriously inconvenience pedestrians, people in wheelchairs or with visual impairments and people with prams or pushchairs.
Law GL(GP)A sect 15

245 **Controlled Parking Zones.** The zone entry signs indicate the times when the waiting restrictions within the zone are in force. Parking may be allowed in some places at other times. Otherwise parking will be within separately signed and marked bays.

246 **Goods vehicles.** Vehicles with a maximum laden weight of over 7.5 tonnes (including any trailer) **MUST NOT** be parked on a verge, pavement or any land situated between carriageways, without police permission. The only exception is when parking is essential for loading and unloading, in which case the vehicle **MUST NOT** be left unattended.
Law RTA 1988 sect 19

247 **Loading and unloading.** Do not load or unload where there are yellow markings on the kerb and upright signs advise restrictions are in place (see pages 109–110). This may be permitted where parking is otherwise restricted. On red routes, specially marked and signed bays indicate where and when loading and unloading is permitted.

Law RTRA sects 5 & 8

Parking at night

248 You **MUST NOT** park on a road at night facing against the direction of the traffic flow unless in a recognised parking space.

Laws CUR reg 101 & RVLR reg 24

249 All vehicles **MUST** display parking lights when parked on a road or a lay-by on a road with a speed limit greater than 30 mph (48 km/h).

Law RVLR reg 24

250 Cars, goods vehicles not exceeding 1525 kg unladen weight, invalid carriages, motorcycles and pedal cycles may be parked without lights on a road (or lay-by) with a speed limit of 30 mph (48 km/h) or less if they are

- at least 10 metres (32 feet) away from any junction, close to the kerb and facing in the direction of the traffic flow
- in a recognised parking place or lay-by.

Other vehicles and trailers, and all vehicles with projecting loads, MUST NOT be left on a road at night without lights.

Laws RVLR reg 24 & CUR reg 82(7)

251 **Parking in fog.** It is especially dangerous to park on the road in fog. If it is unavoidable, leave your parking lights or sidelights on.

252 **Parking on hills.** If you park on a hill you should

- ○ park close to the kerb and apply the handbrake firmly
- ○ select a forward gear and turn your steering wheel away from the kerb when facing uphill
- ○ select reverse gear and turn your steering wheel towards the kerb when facing downhill
- ○ use 'park' if your car has an automatic gearbox.

facing downhill

facing uphill

Rule 252 – *Turn your wheels away from the kerb when parking facing uphill. Turn them towards the kerb when parking facing downhill*

Decriminalised Parking Enforcement (DPE)

DPE is becoming increasingly common as more authorities take on this role. The local traffic authority assumes responsibility for enforcing many parking contraventions in place of the police. Further details on DPE may be found at the following websites:

www.parking-appeals.gov.uk (outside London)
www.parkingandtrafficappeals.gov.uk (inside London)

Motorways

Many other Rules apply to motorway driving, either wholly or in part: Rules 46, 57, 83–126, 130–134, 139, 144, 146–151, 160, 161, 219, 221–222, 225, 226–237, 274–278, 280, and 281–290.

General

253 **Prohibited vehicles.** Motorways **MUST NOT** be used by pedestrians, holders of provisional motorcycle or car licences, riders of motorcycles under 50 cc, cyclists, horse riders, certain slow-moving vehicles and those carrying oversized loads (except by special permission), agricultural vehicles, and powered wheelchairs/powered mobility scooters (see Rules 36–46 incl)
Laws HA 1980 sects 16, 17 & sch 4, MT(E&W)R regs 3(d), 4 & 11, MT(E&W)(A)R, R(S)A sects 7, 8 & sch 3, RTRA sects 17(2) & (3), & MT(S)R reg 10

254 Traffic on motorways usually travels faster than on other roads, so you have less time to react. It is especially important to use your mirrors earlier and look much further ahead than you would on other roads.

Motorway signals

255 Motorway signals (see page 96) are used to warn you of a danger ahead. For example, there may be an incident, fog, a spillage or road workers on the carriageway which you may not immediately be able to see.

256 Signals situated on the central reservation apply to all lanes. On very busy stretches, signals may be overhead with a separate signal for each lane.

257 **Amber flashing lights.** These warn of a hazard ahead. The signal may show a temporary maximum speed limit, lanes that are closed or a message such as 'Fog'. Adjust your speed and look out for the danger until you pass a signal which is not flashing or one that gives the 'All clear' sign and you are sure it is safe to increase your speed.

258 **Red flashing lights.** If red lights on the overhead signals flash above your lane and a red 'X' is showing, you **MUST NOT** go beyond the signal in that lane. If red lights flash on a signal in the central reservation or at the side of the road, you **MUST NOT** go beyond the signal in any lane.

Laws RTA 1988 sect 36 & TSRGD regs 10 & 38

Driving on the motorway

259 **Joining the motorway.** When you join the motorway you will normally approach it from a road on the left (a slip road) or from an adjoining motorway. You should

- ◯ give priority to traffic already on the motorway
- ◯ check the traffic on the motorway and match your speed to fit safely into the traffic flow in the left-hand lane
- ◯ not cross solid white lines that separate lanes or use the hard shoulder
- ◯ stay on the slip road if it continues as an extra lane on the motorway
- ◯ remain in the left-hand lane long enough to adjust to the speed of traffic before considering overtaking.

On the motorway

260 When you can see well ahead and the road conditions are good, you should

- ◯ drive at a steady cruising speed which you and your vehicle can handle safely and is within the speed limit (see table on page 37)
- ◯ keep a safe distance from the vehicle in front and increase the gap on wet or icy roads, or in fog (see Rules 126 and 235).

261 You **MUST NOT** exceed 70 mph (112 km/h), or the maximum speed limit permitted for your vehicle (see page 37). If a lower speed limit is in force, either permanently or temporarily, at road works for example, you **MUST NOT** exceed the lower limit. On some motorways, mandatory motorway signals (which display the speed within a red ring) are used to vary the maximum speed limit to improve traffic flow. You **MUST NOT** exceed this speed limit.

Law RTRA sects 17, 86, 89 & sch 6

The monotony of driving on a motorway can make you feel sleepy. To minimise the risk, follow the advice in Rule 91.

 You **MUST NOT** reverse, cross the central reservation, or drive against the traffic flow. If you have missed your exit, or have taken the wrong route, carry on to the next exit.

Laws MT(E&W)R regs 6, 8 & 10 & MT(S)R regs 4, 5, 7 & 9

Lane discipline

 You should always drive in the left-hand lane when the road ahead is clear. If you are overtaking a number of slower-moving vehicles, you should return to the left-hand lane as soon as you are safely past. Slow-moving or speed-restricted vehicles should always remain in the left-hand lane of the carriageway unless overtaking. You **MUST NOT** drive on the hard shoulder except in an emergency or if directed to do so by the police, HA traffic officers in uniform or by signs.

Laws MT(E&W)R regs 5, 9 & 16(1)(a), MT(S)R regs 4, 8 & 14(1)(a), and RTA 1988, sects 35 & 186, as amended by TMA 2004 sect 6

 The right-hand lane of a motorway with three or more lanes **MUST NOT** be used (except in prescribed circumstances) if you are driving

- ⟳ any vehicle drawing a trailer
- ⟳ a goods vehicle with a maximum laden weight exceeding 3.5 tonnes but not exceeding 7.5 tonnes, which is required to be fitted with a speed limiter
- ⟳ a goods vehicle with a maximum laden weight exceeding 7.5 tonnes
- ⟳ a passenger vehicle with a maximum laden weight exceeding 7.5 tonnes constructed or adapted to carry more than eight seated passengers in addition to the driver
- ⟳ a passenger vehicle with a maximum laden weight not exceeding 7.5 tonnes which is constructed or adapted to carry more than eight seated passengers in addition to the driver, which is required to be fitted with a speed limiter.

Laws MT(E&W)R reg 12, MT(E&W)AR (2004), MT(S)R reg 11 & MT(S)AR (2004)

266 **Approaching a junction.** Look well ahead for signals or signs. Direction signs may be placed over the road. If you need to change lanes, do so in good time. At some junctions a lane may lead directly off the motorway. Only get in that lane if you wish to go in the direction indicated on the overhead signs.

Overtaking

267 Do not overtake unless you are sure it is safe and legal to do so. Overtake only on the right. You should

 check your mirrors

○ take time to judge the speeds correctly

○ make sure that the lane you will be joining is sufficiently clear ahead and behind

○ take a quick sideways glance into the blind spot area to verify the position of a vehicle that may have disappeared from your view in the mirror

○ remember that traffic may be coming up behind you very quickly. Check all your mirrors carefully. Look out for motorcyclists. When it is safe to do so, signal in plenty of time, then move out

○ ensure you do not cut in on the vehicle you have overtaken

○ be especially careful at night and in poor visibility when it is harder to judge speed and distance.

268 Do not overtake on the left or move to a lane on your left to overtake. In congested conditions, where adjacent lanes of traffic are moving at similar speeds, traffic in left-hand lanes may sometimes be moving faster than traffic to the right. In these conditions you may keep up with the traffic in your lane even if this means passing traffic in the lane to your right. Do not weave in and out of lanes to overtake.

269 **Hard shoulder.** You **MUST NOT** use the hard shoulder for overtaking. In areas where an Active Traffic Management (ATM) Scheme is in force, the hard shoulder may be used as a running lane. You will know when you can use this because a speed limit sign will be shown above all open lanes, including the hard shoulder. A red cross or blank sign above the hard shoulder means that you **MUST NOT** drive on the hard shoulder except in an emergency or breakdown. Emergency refuge areas have also been built into these areas for use in cases of emergency or breakdown.

Laws MT(E&W)R regs 5, 5A & 9, MT(S)R regs 4 & 8

Rule 269 – *Overhead gantry showing red cross over hard shoulder*

Stopping

270 You **MUST NOT** stop on the carriageway, hard shoulder, slip road, central reservation or verge except in an emergency, or when told to do so by the police, HA traffic officers in uniform, an emergency sign or by flashing red light signals. Do not stop on the hard shoulder to either make or receive mobile phone calls.

Laws MT(E&W)R regs 5A, 7, 9, 10 & 16,MT(S)R regs 6(1), 8, 9 & 14, PRA 2002 sect 41 & sched 5(8), & RTA 1988 sects 35 & 163 as amended by TMA 2004, sect 6

271 You **MUST NOT** pick up or set down anyone, or walk on a motorway, except in an emergency.

Laws RTRA sect 17 & MT(E&W)R reg 15

Leaving the motorway

272 Unless signs indicate that a lane leads directly off the motorway, you will normally leave the motorway by a slip road on your left. You should

- ◯ watch for the signs letting you know you are getting near your exit
- ◯ move into the left-hand lane well before reaching your exit
- ◯ signal left in good time and reduce your speed on the slip road as necessary.

273 On leaving the motorway or using a link road between motorways, your speed may be higher than you realise – 50 mph may feel like 30 mph. Check your speedometer and adjust your speed accordingly. Some slip-roads and link roads have sharp bends, so you will need to slow down.

Breakdowns & incidents

Breakdowns

274 If your vehicle breaks down, think first of all other road users and

- ◯ get your vehicle off the road if possible
- ◯ warn other traffic by using your hazard warning lights if your vehicle is causing an obstruction
- ◯ help other road users see you by wearing light-coloured or fluorescent clothing in daylight and reflective clothing at night or in poor visibility
- ◯ put a warning triangle on the road at least 45 metres (147 feet) behind your broken-down vehicle on the same side of the road, or use other permitted warning devices if you have them. Always take great care when placing or retrieving them, but never use them on motorways
- ◯ if possible, keep your sidelights on if it is dark or visibility is poor
- ◯ do not stand (or let anybody else stand) between your vehicle and oncoming traffic
- ◯ at night or in poor visibility do not stand where you will prevent other road users seeing your lights.

Additional rules for the motorway

275 If your vehicle develops a problem, leave the motorway at the next exit or pull into a service area. If you cannot do so, you should

- ◯ pull on to the hard shoulder and stop as far to the left as possible, with your wheels turned to the left
- ◯ try to stop near an emergency telephone (situated at approximately one-mile intervals along the hard shoulder)
- ◯ leave the vehicle by the left-hand door and ensure your passengers do the same. You **MUST** leave any animals in the vehicle or, in an emergency, keep them under proper control on the verge. Never attempt to place a warning triangle on a motorway

Rule 275 – *Keep well back from the hard shoulder*

- do not put yourself in danger by attempting even simple repairs
- ensure that passengers keep away from the carriageway and hard shoulder, and that children are kept under control
- walk to an emergency telephone on your side of the carriageway (follow the arrows on the posts at the back of the hard shoulder) – the telephone is free of charge and connects directly to the Highways Agency or the police. Use these in preference to a mobile phone (see Rule 283). Always face the traffic when you speak on the phone
- give full details to the Highways Agency or the police; also inform them if you are a vulnerable motorist such as disabled, older or travelling alone
- return and wait near your vehicle (well away from the carriageway and hard shoulder)
- if you feel at risk from another person, return to your vehicle by a left-hand door and lock all doors. Leave your vehicle again as soon as you feel this danger has passed.

Laws MT(E&W)R reg 14 & MT(S)R reg 12

276 Before you rejoin the carriageway after a breakdown, build up speed on the hard shoulder and watch for a safe gap in the traffic. Be aware that other vehicles may be stationary on the hard shoulder.

277 If you cannot get your vehicle onto the hard shoulder

- do not attempt to place any warning device on the carriageway
- switch on your hazard warning lights
- leave your vehicle only when you can safely get clear of the carriageway.

278 **Disabled drivers.** If you have a disability which prevents you from following the above advice you should

- stay in your vehicle
- switch on your hazard warning lights
- display a 'Help' pennant or, if you have a car or mobile telephone, contact the emergency services and be prepared to advise them of your location.

Obstructions

279 If anything falls from your vehicle (or any other vehicle) on to the road, stop and retrieve it only if it is safe to do so.

280 **Motorways.** On a motorway do not try to remove the obstruction yourself. Stop at the next emergency telephone and call the Highways Agency or the police.

Incidents

281 **Warning signs or flashing lights.** If you see or hear emergency or incident support vehicles in the distance, be aware there may be an incident ahead (see Rule 219). Police Officers and Highways Agency Traffic Officers may be required to work in the carriageway, for example dealing with debris, collisions or conducting rolling road blocks. Police officers will use rear-facing flashing red and blue lights and HA Traffic Officers will use rear-facing flashing red and amber lights in these situations. Watch out for such signals, slow down and be prepared to stop. You **MUST** follow any directions given by Police officers or Traffic officers as to whether you can safely pass the incident or blockage.

Laws RTA1988, sects 35 &163, and as amended by TMA 2004, sect 6

282 When passing the scene of an incident or crash do not be distracted or slow down unnecessarily (for example if an incident is on the other side of a dual carriageway). This may cause a collision or traffic congestion, but see Rule 283.

283 If you are involved in a crash or stop to give assistance

- use your hazard warning lights to warn other traffic
- ask drivers to switch off their engines and stop smoking
- arrange for the emergency services to be called immediately with full details of the incident location and any casualties (on a motorway, use the emergency telephone which allows easy location by the emergency services. If you use a mobile phone, first make sure you have identified your location from the marker posts on the side of the hard shoulder)
- move uninjured people away from the vehicles to safety; on a motorway this should, if possible, be well away from the traffic, the hard shoulder and the central reservation
- do not move injured people from their vehicles unless they are in immediate danger from fire or explosion
- do not remove a motorcyclist's helmet unless it is essential to do so
- be prepared to give first aid as shown on pages 125–127
- stay at the scene until emergency services arrive.

If you are involved in any other medical emergency on the motorway you should contact the emergency services in the same way.

Incidents involving dangerous goods

284 Vehicles carrying dangerous goods in packages will be marked with plain orange reflective plates. Road tankers and vehicles carrying tank containers of dangerous goods will have hazard warning plates (see page 111).

285 If an incident involves a vehicle containing dangerous goods, follow the advice in Rule 283 and, in particular

 switch off engines and **DO NOT SMOKE**

- keep well away from the vehicle and do not be tempted to try to rescue casualties as you yourself could become one
- call the emergency services and give as much information as possible about the labels and markings on the vehicle. **DO NOT** use a mobile phone close to a vehicle carrying flammable loads.

Documentation

286 If you are involved in a collision which causes damage or injury to any other person, vehicle, animal or property, you **MUST**

- stop
- give your own and the vehicle owner's name and address, and the registration number of the vehicle, to anyone having reasonable grounds for requiring them
- if you do not give your name and address at the time of the collision, report it to the police as soon as reasonably practicable, and in any case within 24 hours.

Law RTA 1988 sect 170

287 If another person is injured and you do not produce your insurance certificate at the time of the crash to a police officer or to anyone having reasonable grounds to request it, you **MUST**

- report it to the police as soon as possible and in any case within 24 hours
- produce your insurance certificate for the police within seven days.

Law RTA 1988 sect 170

Road works

288 When the 'Road Works Ahead' sign is displayed, you will need to be more watchful and look for additional signs providing more specific instructions. Observe all signs – they are there for your safety and the safety of road workers.

- You **MUST NOT** exceed any temporary maximum speed limit.
- Use your mirrors and get into the correct lane for your vehicle in good time and as signs direct.
- Do not switch lanes to overtake queuing traffic.
- Take extra care near cyclists and motorcyclists as they are vulnerable to skidding on grit, mud or other debris at road works.
- Where lanes are restricted due to road works, merge in turn (see Rule 134).
- Do not drive through an area marked off by traffic cones.
- Watch out for traffic entering or leaving the works area, but do not be distracted by what is going on there. Concentrate on the road ahead, not the road works.
- Bear in mind that the road ahead may be obstructed by the works or by slow moving or stationary traffic.
- Keep a safe distance – there could be queues in front.

To obtain further information about road works see page 129.

Law RTRA sect 16

Additional rules for high-speed roads

 Take special care on motorways and other high-speed dual carriageways.

- ⮌ One or more lanes may be closed to traffic and a lower speed limit may apply.
- ⮌ Works vehicles that are slow moving or stationary with a large 'Keep Left' or 'Keep Right' sign on the back are sometimes used to close lanes for repairs, and a flashing light arrow may also be used to make the works vehicle more conspicuous from a distance and give earlier warning to drivers that they need to move over to the next lane.
- ⮌ Check mirrors, slow down and change lanes if necessary.
- ⮌ Keep a safe distance from the vehicle in front (see Rule 126).

 Contraflow systems mean that you may be travelling in a narrower lane than normal and with no permanent barrier between you and oncoming traffic. The hard shoulder may be used for traffic, but be aware that there may be broken-down vehicles ahead of you. Keep a good distance from the vehicle ahead and observe any temporary speed limits.

Level crossings

291 A level crossing is where a road crosses a railway or tramway line. Approach and cross it with care. Never drive onto a crossing until the road is clear on the other side and do not get too close to the car in front. Never stop or park on, or near, a crossing.

292 **Overhead electric lines.** It is dangerous to touch overhead electric lines. You **MUST** obey the safe height warning road signs and you should not continue forward onto the railway if your vehicle touches any height barrier or bells. The clearance available is usually 5 metres (16 feet 6 inches) but may be lower.
Laws RTA 1988 sect 36, TSRGD 2002 reg 17(5)

293 **Controlled Crossings.** Most crossings have traffic light signals with a steady amber light, twin flashing red stop lights (see pages 96 & 103) and an audible alarm for pedestrians. They may have full, half or no barriers.

- You **MUST** always obey the flashing red stop lights.
- You **MUST** stop behind the white line across the road.
- Keep going if you have already crossed the white line when the amber light comes on.
- Do not reverse onto or over a controlled crossing.
- You **MUST** wait if a train goes by and the red lights continue to flash. This means another train will be passing soon.
- Only cross when the lights go off and barriers open.
- Never zig-zag around half-barriers, they lower automatically because a train is approaching.
- At crossings where there are no barriers, a train is approaching when the lights show.
Laws RTA 1988 sect 36 & TSRGD regs 10 & 40

***Rule 293** – Stop when the traffic lights show*

294 **Railway telephones.** If you are driving a large or slow-moving vehicle, a long, low vehicle with a risk of grounding, or herding animals, a train could arrive before you are clear of the crossing. You **MUST** obey any sign instructing you to use the railway telephone to obtain permission to cross. You **MUST** also telephone when clear of the crossing if requested to do so.

Laws RTA 1988 sect 36 & TSRGD regs 10 & 16(1)

295 **Crossings without traffic lights.** Vehicles should stop and wait at the barrier or gate when it begins to close and not cross until the barrier or gate opens.

296 **User-operated gates or barriers.** Some crossings have 'Stop' signs and small red and green lights. You **MUST NOT** cross when the red light is showing, only cross if the green light is on. If crossing with a vehicle, you should

- ⤷ open the gates or barriers on both sides of the crossing
- ⤷ check that the green light is still on and cross quickly
- ⤷ close the gates or barriers when you are clear of the crossing.

Laws RTA 1988 sect 36 & TSRGD regs 10 & 52(2)

297 If there are no lights, follow the procedure in Rule 295. Stop, look both ways and listen before you cross. If there is a railway telephone, always use it to contact the signal operator to make sure it is safe to cross. Inform the signal operator again when you are clear of the crossing.

298 **Open crossings.** These have no gates, barriers, attendant or traffic lights but will have a 'Give Way' sign. You should look both ways, listen and make sure there is no train coming before you cross.

299 **Incidents and breakdowns.** If your vehicle breaks down, or if you have an incident on a crossing you should

- ⤷ get everyone out of the vehicle and clear of the crossing immediately
- ⤷ use a railway telephone if available to tell the signal operator. Follow the instructions you are given
- ⤷ move the vehicle clear of the crossing if there is time before a train arrives. If the alarm sounds, or the amber light comes on, leave the vehicle and get clear of the crossing immediately.

Tramways

300 You **MUST NOT** enter a road, lane or other route reserved for trams. Take extra care where trams run along the road. You should avoid driving directly on top of the rails and should take care where trams leave the main carriageway to enter the reserved route, to ensure you do not follow them. The width taken up by trams is often shown by tram lanes marked by white lines, yellow dots or by a different type of road surface. Diamond-shaped signs and white light signals give instructions to tram drivers only.
Law RTRA sects 5 & 8

301 Take extra care where the track crosses from one side of the road to the other and where the road narrows and the tracks come close to the kerb. Tram drivers usually have their own traffic signals and may be permitted to move when you are not. Always give way to trams. Do not try to race or overtake them or pass them on the inside, unless they are at tram stops or stopped by tram signals and there is a designated tram lane for you to pass.

302 You **MUST NOT** park your vehicle where it would get in the way of trams or where it would force other drivers to do so. Do not stop on any part of a tram track, except in a designated bay where this has been provided alongside and clear of the track. When doing so, ensure that all parts of your vehicle are outside the delineated tram path. Remember that a tram cannot steer round an obstruction.
Law RTRA sects 5 & 8

303 **Tram stops.** Where the tram stops at a platform, either in the middle or at the side of the road, you **MUST** follow the route shown by the road signs and markings. At stops without platforms you **MUST NOT** drive between a tram and the left-hand kerb when a tram has stopped to pick up passengers. If there is no alternative route signed, do not overtake the tram – wait until it moves off.
Law RTRA sects 5 & 8

304 Look out for pedestrians, especially children, running to catch a tram approaching a stop.

305 Always give priority to trams, especially when they signal to pull away from stops, unless it would be unsafe to do so. Remember that they may be carrying large numbers of standing passengers who could be injured if the tram had to make an emergency stop. Look out for people getting off a bus or tram and crossing the road.

306 All road users, but particularly cyclists and motorcyclists, should take extra care when driving or riding close to or crossing the tracks, especially if the rails are wet. You should take particular care when crossing the rails at shallow angles, on bends and at junctions. It is safest to cross the tracks directly at right angles. Other road users should be aware that cyclists and motorcyclists may need more space to cross the tracks safely.

307 **Overhead electric lines.** Tramway overhead wires are normally 5.8 metres above any carriageway, but can be lower. You should ensure that you have sufficient clearance between the wire and your vehicle (including any load you are carrying) before driving under an overhead wire. Drivers of vehicles with extending cranes, booms, tipping apparatus or other types of variable height equipment should ensure that the equipment is fully lowered. Where overhead wires are set lower than 5.8 metres, these will be indicated by height clearance markings – similar to 'low bridge' signs. The height clearances on these plates should be carefully noted and observed. If you are in any doubt as to whether your vehicle will pass safely under the wires, you should always contact the local police or the tramway operator. Never take a chance as this can be extremely hazardous.

Light signals controlling traffic

Traffic Light Signals

RED means 'Stop'. Wait behind the stop line on the carriageway

RED AND AMBER also means 'Stop'. Do not pass through or start until GREEN shows

GREEN means you may go on if the way is clear. Take special care if you intend to turn left or right and give way to pedestrians who are crossing

AMBER means 'Stop' at the stop line. You may go on only if the AMBER appears after you have crossed the stop line or are so close to it that to pull up might cause an accident

A GREEN ARROW may be provided in addition to the full green signal if movement in a certain direction is allowed before or after the full green phase. If the way is clear you may go but only in the direction shown by the arrow. You may do this whatever other lights may be showing. White light signals may be provided for trams

Flashing red lights

Alternately flashing red lights mean YOU MUST STOP

At level crossings, lifting bridges, airfields, fire stations, etc.

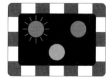

Motorway signals

You **MUST NOT** proceed further in this lane

Change lane

Reduced visibility ahead

Lane ahead closed

Temporary maximum speed advised and information message

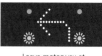

Leave motorway at next exit

Temporary maximum speed advised

End of restriction

Lane control signals

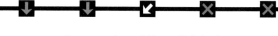

Green arrow – lane available to traffic facing the sign
Red crosses – lane closed to traffic facing the sign
White diagonal arrow – change lanes in direction shown

Signals to other road users

Direction indicator signals

I intend to move out to
the right or turn right

I intend to move in to the left
or turn left or stop on the left

Brake light signals

I am applying the brakes

Reversing light signals

I intend to reverse

These signals should not be used except for the purposes described.

Arm signals

For use when direction indicator signals are not used, or when necessary to reinforce direction
indicator signals and stop lights. **Also for use by pedal cyclists and those in charge of horses.**

I intend to move in to
the left or turn left

I intend to move out to
the right or turn right

I intend to slow down
or stop

Signals by authorised persons

Police officers

Stop

Traffic approaching from the front

Traffic approaching from both front and behind

Traffic approaching from behind

To beckon traffic on

From the side

From the front

From behind*

Arm signals to persons controlling traffic

I want to go straight on

I want to turn left; use either hand

I want to turn right

* In Wales, bilingual signs appear on emergency services vehicles and clothing

Vehicle and Operator Services Agency and Highways Agency Traffic Officers

Highways Agency Traffic Officer

VOSA Traffic Officer

These officers now have new powers to stop/direct vehicles and will be using hand signals and light signals similar to those used by police.
You **MUST** obey any signals given (see Rules 107 and 108).

School Crossing Patrols

Not ready to cross pedestrians

Barrier to stop pedestrians crossing

Ready to cross pedestrians, vehicles must be prepared to stop

All vehicles must stop

Traffic signs

Signs giving orders

Signs with red circles are mostly prohibitive.

Plates below signs qualify their message.

Entry to
20 mph zone

End of
20 mph zone

Maximum
speed

National speed
limit applies

School crossing
patrol

Stop and
give way

Give way to
traffic on
major road

Manually operated temporary
STOP and GO signs

No entry for
vehicular traffic

No vehicles
except bicycles
being pushed

No cycling

No motor
vehicles

No buses
(over 8
passenger
seats)

No
overtaking

No
towed
caravans

No vehicles
carrying
explosives

No vehicle or
combination of
vehicles over
length shown

No vehicles
over
height shown

No vehicles
over
width shown

Give priority to vehicles
from opposite direction

No right turn

No left turn

No
U-turns

No goods vehicles over
maximum gross weight
shown (in tonnes) except
loading and unloading

Note: Although *The Highway Code* shows many of the signs commonly in use, a comprehensive
explanation of our signing system is given in the Department's booklet *Know Your Traffic Signs*,
which is on sale at booksellers. The booklet also illustrates and explains the vast majority of signs
the road user is likely to encounter. The signs illustrated in *The Highway Code* are not all drawn
to the same scale. In Wales, bilingual versions of some signs are used including Welsh and English
versions of place names. Some older designs of signs may still be seen on the roads.

No vehicles over maximum gross weight shown (in tonnes)

Parking restricted to permit holders

No stopping during period indicated except for buses

No stopping during times shown except for as long as necessary to set down or pick up passengers

No waiting

No stopping (Clearway)

Signs with blue circles but no red border mostly give positive instruction.

Ahead only

Turn left ahead (right if symbol reversed)

Turn left (right if symbol reversed)

Keep left (right if symbol reversed)

Vehicles may pass either side to reach same destination

Mini-roundabout (roundabout circulation – give way to vehicles from the immediate right)

Route to be used by pedal cycles only

Segregated pedal cycle and pedestrian route

Minimum speed

End of minimum speed

Buses and cycles only

Trams only

Pedestrian crossing point over tramway

One-way traffic (note: compare circular 'Ahead only' sign)

With-flow bus and cycle lane

Contra-flow bus lane

With-flow pedal cycle lane

Warning signs

Mostly triangular

Distance to 'STOP' line ahead

Dual carriageway ends

Road narrows on right (left if symbol reversed)

Road narrows on both sides

Distance to 'Give Way' line ahead

Crossroads

Junction on bend ahead

T-junction with priority over vehicles from the right

Staggered junction

Traffic merging from left ahead

The priority through route is indicated by the broader line.

Double bend first to left (symbol may be reversed)

Bend to right (or left if symbol reversed)

Roundabout

Uneven road

Plate below some signs

Two-way traffic crosses one-way road

Two-way traffic straight ahead

Opening or swing bridge ahead

Low-flying aircraft or sudden aircraft noise

Falling or fallen rocks

Traffic signals not in use

Traffic signals

Slippery road

Steep hill downwards

Steep hill upwards

Gradients may be shown as a ratio i.e. 20% = 1:5

Tunnel ahead

Trams crossing ahead

Level crossing with barrier or gate ahead

Level crossing without barrier or gate ahead

Level crossing without barrier

School crossing patrol ahead (some signs have amber lights which flash when crossings are in use)

Frail (or blind or disabled if shown) pedestrians likely to cross road ahead

Pedestrians in road ahead

Zebra crossing

Overhead electric cable; plate indicates maximum height of vehicles which can pass safely

Available width of headroom indicated

Sharp deviation of route to left (or right if chevrons reversed)

Light signals ahead at level crossing, airfield or bridge

Miniature warning lights at level crossings

Cattle

Wild animals

Wild horses or ponies

Accompanied horses or ponies

Cycle route ahead

Risk of ice

Traffic queues likely ahead

Distance over which road humps extend

Other danger; plate indicates nature of danger

Soft verges

Side winds

Hump bridge

Worded warning sign

Quayside or river bank

Risk of grounding

Direction signs

Mostly rectangular

Signs on motorways – blue backgrounds

At a junction leading directly
into a motorway (junction
number may be shown
on a black background)

On approaches to
junctions (junction number
on black background)

Route confirmatory
sign after junction

Downward pointing arrows mean 'Get in lane'
The left-hand lane leads to a different destination from the other lanes.

The panel with the inclined arrow indicates the destinations which can be reached
by leaving the motorway at the next junction

Signs on primary routes – green backgrounds

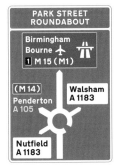

On approaches to
junctions

At the junction

Route confirmatory
sign after junction

On approaches
to junctions

On approach to a junction
in Wales (bilingual)

Blue panels indicate that the motorway starts at the junction ahead.
Motorways shown in brackets can also be reached along the route indicated.
White panels indicate local or non-primary routes leading from the junction ahead.
Brown panels show the route to tourist attractions.
The name of the junction may be shown at the top of the sign.
The aircraft symbol indicates the route to an airport.
A symbol may be included to warn of a hazard or restriction along that route.

Green background signs – continued

Primary route forming part of a ring road

Signs on non-primary and local routes – black borders

On approaches to junctions

At the junction

Direction to toilets with access for the disabled

Green panels indicate that the primary route starts at the junction ahead.
Route numbers on a blue background show the direction to a motorway.
Route numbers on a green background show the direction to a primary route.

Other direction signs

Picnic site

Ancient monument in the care of English Heritage

Direction to a car park

Tourist attraction

Direction to camping and caravan site

Advisory route for lorries

Route for pedal cycles forming part of a network

Recommended route for pedal cycles to place shown

Route for pedestrians

Symbols showing emergency diversion route for motorway and other main road traffic

Diversion route

Information signs

All rectangular

Entrance to controlled parking zone

Entrance to congestion charging zone

End of controlled parking zone

Advance warning of restriction or prohibition ahead

Parking place for solo motorcycles

With-flow bus lane ahead which pedal cycles and taxis may also use

Lane designated for use by high occupancy vehicles (HOV) – see rule 142

Vehicles permitted to use an HOV lane ahead

End of motorway

Start of motorway and point from which motorway regulations apply

Appropriate traffic lanes at junction ahead

Traffic on the main carriageway coming from right has priority over joining traffic

Additional traffic joining from left ahead. Traffic on main carriageway has priority over joining traffic from right-hand lane of slip road

Traffic in right-hand lane of slip road joining the main carriageway has prority over left-hand lane

'Countdown' markers at exit from motorway (each bar represents 100 yards to the exit). Green-backed markers may be used on primary routes and white-backed markers with black bars on other routes. At approaches to concealed level crossings white-backed markers with red bars may be used. Although these will be erected at equal distances the bars do not represent 100 yard intervals.

Motorway service area sign showing the operator's name

Information signs – continued

Priority over oncoming vehicles

Traffic has priority over oncoming vehicles

Hospital ahead with Accident and Emergency facilities

Tourist information point

No through road for vehicles

Recommended route for pedal cycles

Home Zone Entry

Area in which cameras are used to enforce traffic regulations

Bus lane on road at junction ahead

Road works signs

Road works

Loose chippings

Temporary hazard at road works

Temporary lane closure (the number and position of arrows and red bars may be varied according to lanes open and closed)

Slow-moving or stationary works vehicle blocking a traffic lane. Pass in the direction shown by the arrow.

Mandatory speed limit ahead

Road works 1 mile ahead

End of road works and any temporary restrictions including speed limits

Signs used on the back of slow-moving or stationary vehicles warning of a lane closed ahead by a works vehicle. There are no cones on the road.

Lane restrictions at road works ahead

One lane crossover at contraflow road works

Road markings

Across the carriageway

Stop line at signals or police control

Stop line at 'Stop' sign

Stop line for pedestrians at a level crossing

Give way to traffic on major road (can also be used at mini roundabouts)

Give way to traffic from the right at a roundabout

Give way to traffic from the right at a mini-roundabout

Along the carriageway

Edge line

Centre line
See Rule 127

Hazard warning line
See Rule 127

Double white lines
See Rules 128 and 129

See Rule 130

Lane line See Rule 131

Along the edge of the carriageway

Waiting restrictions

Waiting restrictions indicated by yellow lines apply to the carriageway, pavement and verge. You may stop to load or unload (unless there are also loading restrictions as described below) or while passengers board or alight. Double yellow lines mean no waiting at any time, unless there are signs that specifically indicate seasonal restrictions. The times at which the restrictions apply for other road markings are shown on nearby plates or on entry signs to controlled parking zones. If no days are shown on the signs, the restrictions are in force every day including Sundays and Bank Holidays. White bay markings and upright signs (see below) indicate where parking is allowed.

No waiting
at any time

No waiting
during times
shown on sign

Waiting is limited to the
duration specified during the
days and times shown

Red Route stopping controls

Red lines are used on some roads instead of yellow lines. In London the double and single red lines used on Red Routes indicate that stopping to park, load/unload or to board and alight from a vehicle (except for a licensed taxi or if you hold a Blue Badge) is prohibited. The red lines apply to the carriageway, pavement and verge. The times that the red line prohibitions apply are shown on nearby signs, but the double red line ALWAYS means no stopping at any time. On Red Routes you may stop to park, load/unload in specially marked boxes and adjacent signs specify the times and purposes and duration allowed. A box MARKED IN RED indicates that it may only be available for the purpose specified for part of the day (eg between busy peak periods). A box MARKED IN WHITE means that it is available throughout the day.

RED AND SINGLE YELLOW LINES CAN ONLY GIVE A GUIDE TO THE RESTRICTIONS AND CONTROLS IN FORCE AND SIGNS, NEARBY OR AT A ZONE ENTRY, MUST BE CONSULTED.

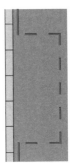

No stopping
at any time

No stopping
during times
shown on sign

Parking is limited to the
duration specified during
the days and times
shown

Only loading may take
place at the times shown
for up to a maximum
duration of 20 mins

On the kerb or at the edge of the carriageway

Loading restrictions on roads other than Red Routes

Yellow marks on the kerb or at the edge of the carriageway indicate that loading or unloading is prohibited at the times shown on the nearby black and white plates. You may stop while passengers board or alight. If no days are indicated on the signs the restrictions are in force every day including Sundays and Bank Holidays.

ALWAYS CHECK THE TIMES SHOWN ON THE PLATES.

Lengths of road reserved for vehicles loading and unloading are indicated by a white 'bay' marking with the words 'Loading Only' and a sign with the white on blue 'trolley' symbol. This sign also shows whether loading and unloading is restricted to goods vehicles and the times at which the bay can be used. If no times or days are shown it may be used at any time. Vehicles may not park here if they are not loading or unloading.

No loading or
unloading
at any time

No loading or
unloading
at the times shown

Loading bay

Other road markings

Keep entrance clear of stationary vehicles, even if picking up or setting down children

Warning of 'Give Way'
just ahead

Parking space reserved
for vehicles named

See Rule 243

See Rule 141

Box junction – See
Rule 174

Do not block that part of
the carriageway indicated

Indication of traffic
lanes

Vehicle markings

Large goods vehicle rear markings

Motor vehicles over 7500 kilograms maximum gross weight and trailers over 3500 kilograms maximum gross weight

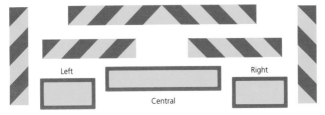

Left

Right

Central

The vertical markings are also required to be fitted to builders' skips placed in the road, commercial vehicles or combinations longer than 13 metres (optional on combinations between 11 and 13 metres)

Hazard warning plates

Certain tank vehicles carrying dangerous goods must display hazard information panels

2YE
1089
Newtown-on-Moors
(0123) 45678

FLAMMABLE LIQUID
3

The panel illustrated is for flammable liquid. Diamond symbols indicating other risks include:

The above panel will be displayed by vehicles carrying certain dangerous goods in packages

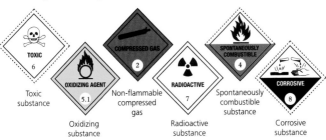

TOXIC
6
Toxic substance

OXIDIZING AGENT
5.1
Oxidizing substance

COMPRESSED GAS
2
Non-flammable compressed gas

RADIOACTIVE
7
Radioactive substance

SPONTANEOUSLY COMBUSTIBLE
4
Spontaneously combustible substance

CORROSIVE
8
Corrosive substance

Projection markers

Side marker

End marker

Both required when load or equipment (eg crane jib) overhangs front or rear by more than two metres

Other

School bus
(displayed in front or rear window of bus or coach)

Annexes

1. You and your bicycle

Make sure that you feel confident of your ability to ride safely on the road. Be sure that

- ↪ you choose the right size and type of cycle for comfort and safety
- ↪ lights and reflectors are kept clean and in good working order
- ↪ tyres are in good condition and inflated to the pressure shown on the tyre
- ↪ gears are working correctly
- ↪ the chain is properly adjusted and oiled
- ↪ the saddle and handlebars are adjusted to the correct height.

It is recommended that you fit a bell to your cycle.

You **MUST**

- ↪ ensure your brakes are efficient
- ↪ at night, use lit front and rear lights and have a red rear reflector.

Laws PCUR regs 6 & 10 & RVLR reg 18

Cycle training can help both children and adults, especially those adults returning to cycling to develop the skills needed to cycle safely on today's roads. A new national cycle training standard has been developed which the Government is promoting and making funding available for delivery in schools.

All cyclists should consider the benefits of undertaking cycle training. For information, contact your local authority.

2. Motorcycle licence requirements

If you have a provisional motorcycle licence, you **MUST** satisfactorily complete a Compulsory Basic Training (CBT) course. You can then ride on the public road, with L plates (in Wales either D plates, L plates or both can be used), for up to two years. To obtain your full motorcycle licence you **MUST** pass a motorcycle theory test and then a practical test.

Law MV(DL)R regs 16 & 68

If you have a full car licence you may ride motorcycles up to 125 cc and 11 kW power output, with L plates (and/or D plates in Wales), on public roads, but you **MUST** first satisfactorily complete a CBT course if you have not already done so.
Law MV(DL)R reg 43

If you have a full moped licence and wish to obtain full motorcycle entitlement, you will be required to take a motorcycle theory test if you did not take a separate theory test when you obtained your moped licence. You **MUST** then pass a practical motorcycle test. Note that if CBT was completed for the full moped licence there is no need to repeat it, but if the moped test was taken before 1/12/90 CBT will need to be completed before riding a motorcycle as a learner.
Law MV(DL)R regs 42(1) & 69(1)

Light motorcycle licence (A1): you take a test on a motorcycle of between 75 and 125 cc. If you pass you may ride a motorcycle up to 125 cc with power output up to 11 kW.

Standard motorcycle licence (A): if your test vehicle is between 120 and 125 cc and capable of more than 100 km/h you will be given a standard (A) licence. You will then be restricted to motorcycles of up to 25 kW for two years. After two years you may ride any size machine.

Direct or Accelerated Access enables riders over the age of 21, or those who reach 21 before their two-year restriction ends, to ride larger motorcycles sooner. To obtain a licence to do so they are required to

- have successfully completed a CBT course
- pass a theory test, if they are required to do so
- pass a practical test on a machine with power output of at least 35 kW.

To practise, they can ride larger motorcycles, with L plates (and/or D plates in Wales), on public roads, but only when accompanied by an approved instructor on another motorcycle in radio contact.

You **MUST NOT** carry a pillion passenger or pull a trailer until you have passed your test.
Law MV(DL)R reg 16

Moped licence requirements

A moped **MUST** have an engine capacity not exceeding 50 cc, not weigh more than 250 kg and be designed to have a maximum speed not exceeding 31 mph (50 km/h). From June 2003 all EC Type Approved mopeds have been restricted to 28 mph (45 km/h).

Law RTA 1988 (as amended) sect 108

To ride a moped, learners **MUST**

- be 16 or over
- have a provisional moped licence
- complete CBT training.

You **MUST** first pass the theory test for motorcycles and then the moped practical test to obtain your full moped licence. If you passed your driving test before 1 February 2001 you are qualified to ride a moped without L plates (and/or D plates in Wales), although it is recommended that you complete CBT before riding on the road. If you passed your driving test after this date you **MUST** complete CBT before riding a moped on the road.

Laws RTA 1988 sects 97(e) & 101 & MV(DL)R regs 38(4) & 43

Note. For motorcycle and moped riders wishing to upgrade, the following give exemption from taking the motorcycle theory test

- full A1 motorcycle licence
- full moped licence, if gained after 1/7/96.

Law MV(DL)R reg 42

3. Motor vehicle documentation and learner driver requirements

Documents

Driving licence. You **MUST** have a valid driving licence for the category of motor vehicle you are driving. You **MUST** inform the Driver and Vehicle Licensing Agency (DVLA) if you change your name and/or address.

Law RTA 1988 sects 87 & 99(4)

Holders of non-European Community licences who are now resident in the UK may only drive on that licence for a maximum of 12 months from the date they become resident in this country.

To ensure continuous driving entitlement

- ◑ a British provisional licence should be obtained and a driving test(s) passed before the 12-month period elapses, or
- ◑ in the case of a driver who holds a licence from a country which has been designated in law for licence exchange purposes, the driver should exchange the licence for a British one.

MOT. Cars and motorcycles **MUST** normally pass an MOT test three years from the date of the first registration and every year after that. You **MUST NOT** drive a motor vehicle without an MOT certificate when it should have one. Exceptionally, you may drive to a pre-arranged test appointment or to a garage for repairs required for the test. Driving an unroadworthy motor vehicle may invalidate your insurance.

Law RTA 1988 sects 45, 47, 49 & 53

Insurance. To use a motor vehicle on the road, you **MUST** have a valid insurance policy. This **MUST** at least cover you for injury or damage to a third party while using that motor vehicle. Before driving any motor vehicle, make sure that it has this cover for your use or that your own insurance provides adequate cover. You **MUST NOT** drive a motor vehicle without insurance. Also, be aware that even if a road traffic incident is not your fault, you may still be held liable by insurance companies.

Law RTA 1988 sect 143

Uninsured drivers can now be automatically detected by roadside cameras. Further to the penalties for uninsured driving listed on page 120, an offender's vehicle can now be seized by the Police, taken away and crushed.

Law RTA 1988, sects 165a & 165b

The types of cover available are indicated below:

Third-Party insurance – this is often the cheapest form of insurance, and is the minimum cover required by law. It covers anyone you might injure or whose property you might damage. It does not cover damage to your own motor vehicle or injury to yourself.

Third-Party, Fire and Theft insurance – similar to third-party, but also covers you against your motor vehicle being stolen, or damaged by fire.

Comprehensive insurance – this is the most expensive but the best insurance. Apart from covering other persons and property against injury or damage, it also covers damage to your own motor vehicle, up to the market value of that vehicle, and personal injury to yourself.

Registration certificate. Registration certificates (also called harmonised registration certificates) are issued for all motor vehicles used on the road, describing them (make, model, etc) and giving details of the registered keeper. You **MUST** notify the Driver and Vehicle Licensing Agency in Swansea as soon as possible when you buy or sell a motor vehicle, or if you change your name or address. For registration certificates issued after 27 March 1997, the buyer and seller are responsible for completing the registration certificates. The seller is responsible for forwarding them to DVLA. The procedures are explained on the back of the registration certificates.

Law RV(R&L)R regs 21, 22, 23 & 24

Vehicle Excise Duty (VED). All motor vehicles used or kept on public roads **MUST** display a valid Vehicle Excise Duty disc (tax disc) displayed at all times. Even motor vehicles exempt from duty **MUST** display a tax disc at all times.

Law VERA sects 29 and 33

Statutory Off-Road Notification (SORN). This is a notification to the DVLA that a motor vehicle is not being used on the road. If you are the vehicle keeper and want to keep a motor vehicle untaxed and off the public road you **MUST** declare SORN – it is an offence not to do so. You then won't have to pay any road tax for that vehicle for a period of 12 months. You need to send a further declaration after that period if the vehicle is still off the public road. The SORN will end if you sell the vehicle and the new owner will become immediately responsible.

Law RV(RL)R 2002, reg 26 sched 4

Production of documents. You **MUST** be able to produce your driving licence and counterpart, a valid insurance certificate and (if appropriate) a valid MOT certificate, when requested by a police officer. If you cannot do this you may be asked to take them to a police station within seven days.

Law RTA 1988 sects 164 & 165

Learner drivers

Learners driving a car **MUST** hold a valid provisional licence. They **MUST** be supervised by someone at least 21 years old who holds a full EC/EEA licence for that type of car (automatic or manual) and has held one for at least three years.

Laws MV(DL)R reg 16 & RTA 1988 sect 87

Vehicles. Any vehicle driven by a learner **MUST** display red L plates. In Wales, either red D plates, red L plates, or both, can be used. Plates **MUST** conform to legal specifications and **MUST** be clearly visible to others from in front of the vehicle and from behind. Plates should be removed or covered when not being driven by a learner (except on driving school vehicles).

Law MV(DL)R reg 16 & sched 4

You **MUST** pass the theory test (if one is required) and then a practical driving test for the category of vehicle you wish to drive before driving unaccompanied.

Law MV(DL)R reg 40

4. The road user and the law

Road traffic law

The following list can be found abbreviated throughout the Code. It is not intended to be a comprehensive guide, but a guide to some of the important points of law. For the precise wording of the law, please refer to the various Acts and Regulations (as amended) indicated in the Code. Abbreviations are listed on the following page.

Most of the provisions apply on all roads throughout Great Britain, although there are some exceptions. The definition of a road in England and Wales is 'any highway and any other road to which the public has access and includes bridges over which a road passes' (RTA 1988 sect 192(1)). In Scotland, there is a similar definition which is extended to include any way over which the public have a right of passage (R(S)A 1984 sect 151(1)).

It is important to note that references to 'road' therefore generally include footpaths, bridleways and cycle tracks, and many roadways and driveways on private land (including many car parks). In most cases, the law will apply to them and there may be additional rules for particular paths or ways. Some serious driving offences, including drink-driving offences, also apply to all public places, for example public car parks.

Chronically Sick & Disabled Persons Act 1970	CSDPA
Functions of Traffic Wardens Order 1970	FTWO
Greater London (General Powers) Act 1974	GL(GP)A
Highway Act 1835 or 1980 (as indicated)	HA
Horses (Protective Headgear for Young Riders) Act 1990	H(PHYR)A
Horses (Protective Headgear for Young Riders) Regulations 1992	H(PHYR)R
Motor Cycles (Eye Protectors) Regulations 1999	MC(EP)R
Motor Cycles (Protective Helmets) Regulations 1998	MC(PH)R
Motorways Traffic (England & Wales) Regulations 1982	MT(E&W)R
Motorways Traffic (England & Wales) Amended Regulations	MT(E&W)(A)R
Motorways Traffic (Scotland) Regulations 1995	MT(S)R
Motor Vehicles (Driving Licences) Regulations 1999	MV(DL)R
Motor Vehicles (Wearing of Seat Belts) Regulations 1993	MV(WSB)R
Motor Vehicles (Wearing of Seat Belts) (Amendment) Regulations 2006	MV(WSB)(A)R
Motor Vehicles (Wearing of Seat Belts by Children in Front Seats) Regulations 1993	MV(WSBCFS)R
New Roads and Streetworks Act 1991	NRSWA
Pedal Cycles (Construction & Use) Regulations 1983	PCUR
Powers of Criminal Courts (Sentencing) Act 2000	PCC(S)A
Police Reform Act 2002	PRA
Prohibition of Smoking in Certain Premises (Scotland) Regulations 2006. Scottish SI 2006/No 90	TPSCP(S)R*
Public Passenger Vehicles Act 1981	PPVA
Road Safety Act 2006	RSA
Road Traffic Act 1984, 1988 or 1991 (as indicated)	RTA
Road Traffic (New Drivers) Act 1995	RT(ND)A
Road Traffic Offenders Act 1988	RTOA
Road Traffic Regulation Act 1984	RTRA
Road Vehicles (Construction & Use) Regulations 1986	CUR
Road Vehicles (Display of Registration Marks) Regulations 2001	RV(DRM)R
Road Vehicles Lighting Regulations 1989	RVLR
Road Vehicles (Registration & Licensing) Regulations 2002	RV(R&L)R
Roads (Scotland) Act 1984	R(S)A
Smoke-free (Exemptions and Vehicles) Regulations 2007 SI 2007/765	TSf(EV)*
Smoke-free Premises etc (Wales) Regulations 2007 SI 2007/W787	TSfP(W)R*
Traffic Management Act 2004	TMA
Traffic Signs Regulations & General Directions 2002	TSRGD
Use of Invalid Carriages on Highways Regulations 1988	UICHR
Vehicle Excise and Registration Act 1994	VERA
Zebra, Pelican and Puffin Pedestrian Crossings Regulations and General Directions 1997	ZPPPCRGD

Acts and regulations from 1988 can be viewed on the Office of Public Sector Information website (www.opsi.gov.uk). Acts and regulations prior to 1988 are only available in their original print format which may be obtained from The Stationery Office as detailed inside the back cover.

*Specific legislation applies to smoking in vehicles which constitute workplaces. For information, visit
www.smokefreeengland.co.uk
www.clearingtheairscotland.com
www.smokingbanwales.co.uk

5. Penalties

Parliament sets the maximum penalties for road traffic
offences. The seriousness of the offence is reflected in
the maximum penalty. It is for the courts to decide what
sentence to impose according to circumstances.

The penalty table on page 120 indicates some of the
main offences, and the associated penalties. There is a
wide range of other more specific offences which, for
the sake of simplicity, are not shown here. The penalty
points and disqualification system is described below.

Penalty points and disqualification

The penalty point system is intended to deter drivers
and motorcyclists from following unsafe motoring
practices. Certain non-motoring offences, e.g. failure to
rectify vehicle defects, can also attract penalty points.
The court **MUST** order points to be endorsed on the
licence according to the fixed number or the range set
by Parliament. The accumulation of penalty points acts
as a warning to drivers and motorcyclists that they risk
disqualification if further offences are committed.

Law RTOA sects 44 & 45

A driver or motorcyclist who accumulates 12 or more
penalty points within a three-year period **MUST** be
disqualified. This will be for a minimum period of six
months, or longer if the driver or motorcyclist has
previously been disqualified.

Law RTOA sect 35

For every offence which carries penalty points the court
has a discretionary power to order the licence holder
to be disqualified. This may be for any period the court
thinks fit, but will usually be between a week and
a few months.

In the case of serious offences, such as dangerous
driving and drink-driving, the court **MUST** order
disqualification. The minimum period is 12 months, but
for repeat offenders or where the alcohol level is high,
it may be longer. For example, a second drink-drive
offence in the space of 10 years will result in
a minimum of three years' disqualification.

Law RTOA sect 34

Penalty Table

Offence	Imprisonment	Maximum Penalties Fine	Disqualification	Penalty Points
*causing death by dangerous driving	14 years	Unlimited	Obligatory – 2 years minimum	3–11 (if exceptionally not disqualified)
*Dangerous driving	2 years	Unlimited	Obligatory	3–11 (if exceptionally not disqualified)
*Causing death by careless driving under the influence of drink or drugs	14 years	Unlimited	Obligatory – 2 years minimum	3–11 (if exceptionally not disqualified)
Careless and inconsiderate driving	-	£5,000	Discretionary	3–9
Driving while unfit through drink or drugs or with excess alcohol: or failing to provide a specimen for analysis	6 months	£5,000	Obligatory	3–11 (if exceptionally not disqualified)
Failing to stop after an accident or failing to report an accident	6 months	£5,000	Discretionary	5–10
Driving when disqualified	6 months (12 months in Scotland)	£5,000	Discretionary	6
Driving after refusal or revocation of licence on medical grounds	6 months	£5,000	Discretionary	3–6
Driving without insurance	-	£5,000	Discretionary	6–8
Using a vehicle in a dangerous condition	-	LGV £5,000 PCV £5,000 Other £2,500	Obligatory if offence committed within 3 years of a previous conviction for the same offence – 6 months min otherwise discretionary	3 in each case
Failure to have proper control of vehicle or full view of the road and traffic ahead, or using a hand-held mobile phone while driving	-	£1,000 (£2,500 for PCV or goods vehicle)	Discretionary	3
Driving otherwise than in accordance with a licence	-	£1,000	Discretionary	3–6
Speeding	-	£1,000 (£2,500 for motorway offences)	Discretionary	3–6 or 3 (fixed penalty)
Traffic light offences	-	£1,000	Discretionary	3
No MOT certificate	-	£1,000	-	-
Seat belt offences	-	£500	-	-
Dangerous cycling	-	£2,500	-	-
Careless cycling	-	£1,000	-	-
Cycling on pavement	-	£500	-	-
Failing to identify driver of a vehicle	-	£1,000	Discretionary	6

*Where a court disqualifies a person on conviction for one of these offences, it must order an extended retest. The courts also have discretion to order a retest for any other offence which carries penalty points, an extended retest where disqualification is obligatory, and an ordinary test where disqualification is not obligatory.

Furthermore, in some serious cases, the court **MUST** (in addition to imposing a fixed period of disqualification) order the offender to be disqualified until they pass a driving test. In other cases the court has a discretionary power to order such disqualification. The test may be an ordinary length test or an extended test according to the nature of the offence.

Law RTOA sect 36

New drivers. Special rules as set out below apply for a period of two years from the date of passing their first driving test, to drivers and motorcyclists from

- ↻ the UK, EU/EEA, the Isle of Man, the Channel Islands or Gibraltar who passed their first driving test in any of those countries
- ↻ other foreign countries who have to pass a UK driving test to gain a UK licence, in which case the UK driving test is treated as their first driving test; and
- ↻ other foreign countries who (without needing a test) exchanged their licence for a UK licence and subsequently passed a UK driving test to drive another type of vehicle, in which case the UK driving test is treated as their first driving test. For example a driver who exchanges a foreign licence (car) for a UK licence (car) and who later passes a test to drive another type of vehicle (e.g. an HGV) will be subject to the special rules.

Where a person subject to the special rules accumulates six or more penalty points before the end of the two-year period (including any points acquired before passing the test) their licence will be revoked automatically. To regain the licence they must reapply for a provisional licence and may drive only as a learner until they pass a further driving test (also see Annex 8 – Safety code for new drivers.)

Law RT(ND)A

Note. This applies even if they pay for offences by fixed penalty. Drivers in the first group (UK, EU/EEA etc.) who already have a full licence for one type of vehicle are not affected by the special rules if they later pass a test to drive another type of vehicle.

Other consequences of offending

Where an offence is punishable by imprisonment then the vehicle used to commit the offence may be confiscated.

Law PCC(S)A, sect 143

In addition to the penalties a court may decide to impose, the cost of insurance is likely to rise considerably following conviction for a serious driving offence. This is because insurance companies consider such drivers are more likely to be involved in a collision.

Drivers disqualified for drinking and driving twice within 10 years, or once if they are over two and a half times the legal limit, or those who refused to give a specimen, also have to satisfy the Driver and Vehicle Licensing Agency's Medical Branch that they do not have an alcohol problem and are otherwise fit to drive before their licence is returned at the end of their period of disqualification. Persistent misuse of drugs or alcohol may lead to the withdrawal of a driving licence.

6. Vehicle maintenance, safety and security

Vehicle maintenance
Take special care that lights, brakes, steering, exhaust system, seat belts, demisters, wipers and washers are all working. Also

- lights, indicators, reflectors, and number plates **MUST** be kept clean and clear
- windscreens and windows **MUST** be kept clean and free from obstructions to vision
- lights **MUST** be properly adjusted to prevent dazzling other road users. Extra attention needs to be paid to this if the vehicle is heavily loaded
- exhaust emissions **MUST NOT** exceed prescribed levels
- ensure your seat, seat belt, head restraint and mirrors are adjusted correctly before you drive
- ensure that items of luggage are securely stowed.

Laws RVLR 1989 regs 23 & 27 & CUR 1986, regs 30 & 61

Warning displays. Make sure that you understand the meaning of all warning displays on the vehicle instrument panel. Do not ignore warning signs, they could indicate a dangerous fault developing.

- When you turn the ignition key, warning lights will be illuminated but will go out when the engine starts (except the handbrake warning light). If they do not, or if they come on while you are driving, stop and investigate the problem, as you could have a serious fault.

⊙ If the charge warning light comes on while you are driving, it may mean that the battery isn't charging. This should also be checked as soon as possible to avoid loss of power to lights and other electrical systems.

Window tints. You **MUST NOT** use a vehicle with excessively dark tinting applied to the windscreen, or to the glass in any front window to either side of the driver. Window tinting applied during manufacture complies with the Visual Light Transmittance (VLT) standards. There are no VLT limits for rear windscreens or rear passenger windows.
Laws RTA 1988 sect 42 & CUR reg 32

Tyres. Tyres MUST be correctly inflated to the vehicle manufacturer's specification for the load being carried. Always refer to the vehicle's handbook or data. Tyres should also be free from certain cuts and other defects.

Cars, light vans and light trailers **MUST** have a tread depth of at least 1.6 mm across the central three-quarters of the breadth of the tread and around the entire circumference.

Motorcycles, large vehicles and passenger-carrying vehicles **MUST** have a tread depth of at least 1 mm across three-quarters of the breadth of the tread and in a continuous band around the entire circumference.

Mopeds should have visible tread.

Be aware that some vehicle defects can attract penalty points.
Law CUR reg 27

If a tyre bursts while you are driving, try to keep control of your vehicle. Grip the steering wheel firmly and allow the vehicle to roll to a stop at the side of the road.

If you have a flat tyre, stop as soon as it is safe to do so. Only change the tyre if you can do so without putting yourself or others at risk – otherwise call a breakdown service.

Tyre pressures. Check weekly. Do this before your journey, when tyres are cold. Warm or hot tyres may give a misleading reading.

Your brakes and steering will be adversely affected by under-inflated or over-inflated tyres. Excessive or uneven tyre wear may be caused by faults in the braking or suspension systems, or wheels which are out of alignment. Have these faults corrected as soon as possible.

Fluid levels. Check the fluid levels in your vehicle at least weekly. Low brake fluid may result in brake failure and a crash. Make sure you recognise the low fluid warning lights if your vehicle has them fitted.

Before winter. Ensure that the battery is well maintained and that there are appropriate anti-freeze agents in your radiator and windscreen bottle.

Other problems. If your vehicle

- pulls to one side when braking, it is most likely to be a brake fault or incorrectly inflated tyres. Consult a garage or mechanic immediately
- continues to bounce after pushing down on the front or rear, its shock absorbers are worn. Worn shock absorbers can seriously affect the operation of a vehicle and should be replaced
- smells of anything unusual such as burning rubber, petrol or an electrical fault; investigate immediately. Do not risk a fire.

Overheated engines or fire. Most engines are water-cooled. If your engine overheats you should wait until it has cooled naturally. Only then remove the coolant filler cap and add water or other coolant.

If your vehicle catches fire, get the occupants out of the vehicle quickly and to a safe place. Do not attempt to extinguish a fire in the engine compartment, as opening the bonnet will make the fire flare. Call the fire brigade.

Petrol stations/fuel tank/fuel leaks. Ensure that, when filling up your vehicle's tank or any fuel cans you are carrying, you do not spill fuel on the forecourt. Any spilled fuel should be immediately reported to the petrol station attendant. Diesel spillage is dangerous to other road users, particularly motorcyclists, as it will significantly reduce the level of grip between the tyres and road surface. Double-check for fuel leaks and make sure that

- you do not overfill your fuel tank
- the fuel cap is fastened securely
- the seal in the cap is not torn, perished or missing
- there is no visual damage to the cap or the fuel tank

Emergency fuel caps, if fitted, should form a good seal.

Never smoke, or use a mobile phone, on the forecourt of petrol stations as these are major fire risks and could cause an explosion.

Vehicle security
When you leave your vehicle you should

- ↻ remove the ignition key and engage the steering lock
- ↻ lock the car, even if you only leave it for a few minutes
- ↻ close the windows completely
- ↻ never leave children or pets in an unventilated car
- ↻ take all contents with you, or lock them in the boot. Remember, for all a thief knows a carrier bag may contain valuables
- ↻ never leave vehicle documents in the car.

For extra security fit an anti-theft device such as an alarm or immobiliser. If you are buying a new car it is a good idea to check the level of built-in security features. Consider having your registration number etched on all your car windows. This is a cheap and effective deterrent to professional thieves.

7. First Aid on the road

In the event of an incident, you can do a number of things to help, even if you have had no training.

1. Deal with danger
Further collisions and fire are the main dangers following a crash. Approach any vehicle involved with care. Switch off all engines and, if possible, warn other traffic. Stop anyone from smoking.

2. Get help
Try to get the assistance of bystanders. Get someone to call the appropriate emergency services as soon as possible. They will need to know the exact location of the incident and the number of vehicles involved.

3. Help those involved
DO NOT move casualties still in vehicles unless further danger is threatened. **DO NOT** remove a motorcyclist's helmet unless it is essential. Remember the casualty may be suffering from shock. **DO NOT** give them anything to eat or drink. **DO** try to make them warm and as comfortable as you can, but avoid unnecessary movement. **DO** give reassurance confidently and try not to leave them alone or let them wander into the path of other traffic.

4. Provide emergency care

Remember the letters **DR A B C:**

D – Danger – check that you are not in danger.
R – Response – try to get a response by asking questions and gently shaking their shoulders.
A – Airway – the airway should be clear and kept open. Place one hand on the forehead, two fingers under the chin and gently tilt the head back.
B – Breathing – normal breathing should be established. Once the airway is open check breathing for up to 10 seconds.
C – Compressions – if they are not breathing normally compressions should be administered to maintain circulation; place two hands in the centre of the chest and press down 4–5 cms at a rate of 100/minute. You may only need one hand for a child. Give 30 chest compressions. Then tilt the head back gently, pinch the casualty's nostrils together and place your mouth over theirs. Give two breaths, each lasting one second (use gentle breaths for a small child).

If the casualty is unconscious and breathing, place them in the recovery position until medical help arrives

Bleeding. First check for anything that may be in the wound, such as glass. If there is nothing embedded apply firm pressure over the wound. Take care not to press on the object – build up padding on either side of it. Fasten a pad to the wound with a bandage or length of cloth. Use the cleanest material available. If a limb is bleeding, but not broken, raise it above the level of the heart to reduce the flow of blood. Any restriction of blood circulation for more than a short time could cause long-term injuries.

Burns. Try to cool the burn by dousing it with clean, cold water or similar non-toxic liquid for at least 10 minutes. Do not try to remove anything sticking to the burn.

5. Be prepared

Always carry a first aid kit. You could save a life by learning emergency aid and first aid from a qualified organisation, such as the local ambulance services, the St John Ambulance Association and Brigade, St Andrew's Ambulance Association, the British Red Cross or any suitable qualified body (see page 129 for contact details).

8. Safety code for new drivers

Once you have passed the driving test you will be able to drive on your own. This will provide you with lots of opportunities but you need to remain safe. Even though you have shown you have the skills you need to drive safely, many newly qualified drivers lack experience. You need to continue to develop your skills, especially anticipating other road users' behaviour to avoid having a collision. As many as one new driver in five has some kind of collision in their first year of driving. This code provides advice to help you get through the first twelve months after passing the driving test, when you are most vulnerable, as safely as possible.

- Many of the worst collisions happen at night. Between midnight and 6 am is a time of high risk for new drivers. Avoid driving then unless it's really necessary.
- If you are driving with passengers, you are responsible for their safety. Don't let them distract you or encourage you to take risks. Tell your passengers that you need to concentrate if you are to get to your destination safely.
- Never show off or try to compete with other drivers, particularly if they are driving badly.
- Don't drive if you have consumed any alcohol or taken drugs. Even over-the-counter medicines can affect your ability to drive safely – read the label to see if they may affect your driving.
- Make sure everyone in the car is wearing a seat belt throughout the journey.
- Keep your speed down – many serious collisions happen because the driver loses control, particularly on bends.

- Most new drivers have no experience of driving high-powered or sporty cars. Unless you have learnt to drive in such a vehicle you need to get plenty of experience driving on your own before driving a more powerful car.
- Driving while uninsured is an offence. See Annex 3 for information on types of insurance cover.

REMEMBER that under the New Drivers Act you will have your licence revoked if you get six penalty points on your licence within two years of passing your first driving test. You will need to pass both the theory and practical tests again to get back your full licence.

You could consider taking further training such as Pass Plus, which could also save you money on your insurance, as well as helping you reduce your risk of being involved in a collision. There are three ways to find out more:

- internet – www.passplus.org.uk
- telephone – DSA head office on 0115 901 2633
- Email – passplus@dsa.gsi.gov.uk

Other information

Metric conversions

The conversions given throughout *The Highway Code* are rounded but a detailed conversion chart is shown below.

Miles	Kilometres	Miles	Kilometres
1.00	1.61	40.00	64.37
5.00	8.05	45.00	72.42
10.00	16.09	50.00	80.47
15.00	24.14	55.00	88.51
20.00	32.19	60.00	96.56
25.00	40.23	65.00	104.60
30.00	48.28	70.00	112.65
35.00	56.33		

Useful websites

www.sja.org.uk   (St John Ambulance Association and Brigade)
www.firstaid.org.uk   (St Andrew's Ambulance Association)
www.redcross.org.uk   (The British Red Cross)
www.dft.gov.uk
www.direct.gov.uk
www.transportoffice.gov.uk
www.highways.gov.uk/traffic info
www.direct.gov.uk/highway code
www.larsoa.org.uk
www.collisionreporting.gov.uk
www.askthe.police.uk
www.parking-appeals.gov.uk (outside London)
www.parkingandtrafficappeals.gov.uk (inside London)

Further reading

Best practice

Further information about good driving and riding practice can be found in The Driving Standards Agency books *The Official DSA Guide to Driving – the essential skills* and *The Official DSA Guide to Riding – the essential skills*. Information specifically for drivers of large vehicles can be found in *The Official DSA Guide to Driving Goods Vehicles* and *The Official DSA Guide to Driving Buses and Coaches*.

The Blue Badge Scheme

Information on this scheme can be found on the Department for Transport Website: www.dft.gov.uk

Code of Practice for Horse-Drawn Vehicles

The Code of Practice is available from the Department for Transport, Transport Technology and Standards Division 6, 2nd Floor, Great Minster House, 76 Marsham Street, London SW1P 4DR.
Tel 0207 944 2078

Road works

A leaflet giving further information on driving through road works can be obtained from Highways Agency Publications, tel 0870 1226 236, quoting reference number HA113/04. For general Highways Agency information, tel 08457 504030 or email ha_info@ highways.gsi.gov.uk

Caring for your bike

Taking the time to look after your motorbike makes a lot of sense. A well-maintained bike is less likely to break down, and it will hold on to more of its value when you come to sell it. Learning to carry out simple maintenance jobs yourself will save you money too. Our guide shows you how.

Cleaning your bike

Cleaning your motorbike regularly helps to protect it from damage and deterioration, and is also vital to preserve your bike's value when you come to sell it.

Giving your bike a thorough wash and brush up isn't just about keeping it clean. It's a chance to give it a really close inspection, which will let you spot small problems before they develop into something more serious. Look carefully for cracks or other damage to the wheels or frame, and for the first signs of corrosion which need to be treated straight away.

Washing

Most bike owners will be happy to use a bucket of water, detergent and a sponge. A pressure washer can be useful if your bike is really filthy, but take care when using it around the bearings as you can easily force out grease which will lead to premature wear. When washing your bike, first remove the thicker oily deposits that will have come from the chain at the

Washing a bike regularly keeps it smart and helps protects its value too

rear. A rag dipped in degreaser or paraffin is best to clean this off. Remember to put on some fresh chain lubricant afterwards to replace any that gets washed away.

The rest of the bike can be washed with warm water and detergent. Use a specialised bike cleaning detergent, rather than washing-up liquid which can be harsh on paintwork.

Use a glass cleaner on the screen, and buff off marks with a soft clean cloth. Don't use the same cloth that you've used to clean mucky bodywork, or pieces of grit hidden in the cloth could leave nasty scratches on the screen.

Brakes

Thick deposits of brake dust will need displacing with a stiff brush (an old toothbrush works fine). Special brake dust removing sprays are available which make the job easier. Clear away dust from inside the brake caliper too, using brake cleaner or fresh brake fluid, but avoid other cleaning products here which might damage the hydraulic seals.

Polishing

A good polish will add extra protection to the paintwork and avoid the need to clean so often in the future. Dry the bodywork thoroughly, before polishing. Use two soft cloths – one for applying the polish, and one for buffing it off. Cotton cloths are best, as they avoid the problem of small particles of cloth sticking to the paint as you polish.

Apply a thin, even layer of polish using a light circular motion, then let it dry to a haze (not a white powder), and lightly buff it off using your buffing cloth. Use a specialised polish on aluminium and chrome finishes.

On an older bike where paintwork has faded, a paint restoring polish can freshen up the finish. Don't overdo it though, as these work by scouring away the faded outer layers of paint, and if used too often you risk removing the paint altogether.

Many specialist products are available to help you keep your bike clean

Maintenance

Routine maintenance is essential to keep your bike in a roadworthy, safe and legal condition. It will save money if you can learn to carry out simple maintenance checks yourself.

Prevention is always better than a cure. So every time you ride your bike, take a quick glance over it to check that there are no obvious faults. Look to see if any nuts and bolts have worked loose, or if the tyres seem low on air or damaged. Make sure that all the lights and the number plate are kept clean at all times. Keep an eye on how your bike performs. At the first sign of any problems, such as rough running, knocking noises, reduced braking performance or a reluctance to start first thing in the morning, get the bike checked out. Don't wait for the problem to get so bad that you end up stranded at the roadside with a broken down bike.

Weekly checks
Once a week, you should carry out a more detailed check of your bike. Use a gauge to check the tyre pressures, and look all over the tyres for cuts and bulges or excessive tread wear. Use the dipstick to check the oil level and top it up if necessary. Also check the levels in the coolant reservoir on a water-cooled engine, and in the brake fluid reservoir. Check if the cables need adjusting, and that wiring to the battery is clean and properly secured. Make sure that all the lights, including the indicators, are working, and test the horn too.

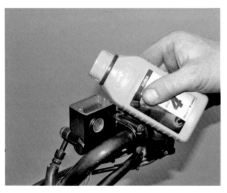

Get into the routine of carrying out regular maintenance checks on your bike

Buy the best quality socket set that you can afford

Tool box

A selection of basic tools is essential if you intend to carry out work on your bike yourself. You don't need the most expensive tools, but generally you get what you pay for. A good quality set will last years, and it can make more sense to buy a good set second-hand than a cheap, low-quality set brand new.

Once you've built up a decent tool kit, make sure you keep it in good condition. Never leave tools lying around after they've been used. Take care when using them, and don't try to use them for a job they're not designed for. The basic tools you will need include:

🜨 Spanners

Sets usually include a full range from 7 to 19mm. It can pay to get pairs of 10, 12 and 13mm spanners as sometimes two are needed to undo a component. If you own an American or older British bike you will need imperial spanners instead.

🜨 Socket set

A good set will include sockets ranging from 6mm to 24mm. For classic bikes, again you will require an imperial set. It can be useful to get Allen, Torx and Spline bits for your socket set to fit the appropriate bolts fitted to your bike.

🜨 Screwdrivers

Get a good selection of screwdrivers with both Phillips and flat blades. Make sure the handles are comfortable and fit your hand snugly.

🜨 Allen keys

Most bikes use Allen bolts, so a good set of keys is essential. Socket Allen keys are useful to loosen tight bolts.

🜨 Pliers

In addition to a standard set of pliers, long-handled snipe-nose pliers are useful when working on a motorbike, as they allow you to reach through narrow gaps.

🜨 Torque wrench

A torque wrench is essential to ensure fasteners are tightened by the correct amount. Look for a torque wrench with a working range of 7–100Nm, as the settings used on bikes are generally lower than those for cars.

Chain care

Chains do a lot of work and can wear rapidly if neglected. Make sure you inspect your bike's chain at least every 600 miles and keep it properly lubricated and adjusted.

Cleaning the chain

You need to keep your bike's chain clean because when grit and dirt sticks to an oily chain it starts to act as a grinding paste, accelerating wear. Use a chain cleaner such as paraffin to remove the accumulated oil and dirt, then rinse it off and let the chain dry thoroughly before applying more lubricant. If you spray on oil when the chain is wet, you can trap in moisture which will cause the chain to rust.

Lubrication

Most motorbikes have O-ring chains, which have rubber seals that keep the lubricant inside the rollers. Use only O-ring chain lube, which is designed to protect the outside of the chain and keep the grease inside.

Aim the lube so it hits in between the plates on both sides of the chain. Applying lube after a ride, when the chain is warm, will help it to penetrate. Wipe away any excess or it will fly off and make a mess when you next ride the bike.

It's worth fitting an automatic oiler which will not only save the effort of lubricating the chain yourself but should also extend the life of the chain considerably.

Never allow the chain to run dry, which would result in a very rapid rate of wear.

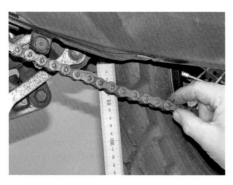

A motorbike chain is a hard-working component and it needs regular maintenance

Keeping the chain correctly adjusted and lubricated will extend its life

Checking chain tension

A loose or worn drive chain is potentially dangerous: it can cause a noisy rattle, affect gear changing and ultimately cause the rear wheel to lock, leading to an accident. A chain that's too tight is also to be avoided, as it may cause damage to the gearbox and wheel bearings.

There should be around three to four centimetres of free play in a chain, but refer to your motorbike's handbook or Haynes Manual for the exact specification. To measure chain tension, with the bike upright and in neutral, push the bottom chain down and measure the slack midway between the two sprockets. Repeat this at several points along the chain as they can wear unevenly.

Adjust so that the tension is correct at the tightest point on the chain. First slacken off the wheel spindle. Then loosen the lock nuts on the sliding adjuster screws and turn them by an equal amount until the chain reaches the correct tension.

Once your chain is so worn that no more adjustment is possible, it needs replacing. To check this, with the chain taut, measure a number of links along the top run and compare this with the figures specified in your manual. If any O-rings have kinked or seized then the chain should be replaced.

Check the sprockets for signs of wear too, and replace any with bent or worn teeth.

Wheel alignment

Once you have adjusted chain tension, you need to check the rear wheel alignment. The wheel alignment marks should be in the same place on both sides. If they are not, push the wheel back or forward until they line up. Then check the chain tension again. Once you are sure that everything is correct, tighten the spindle to the correct torque setting and tighten the locknuts. Make a final check of the chain tension before you ride the bike.

Brakes

Effective brakes are essential for your safety. It's essential to keep them properly maintained so they are in tip-top condition whenever you need to use them in an emergency.

Your bike may be fitted with disc or drum brakes, or a combination of the two. Discs are fitted with pads, drums with shoes, but in both cases they operate in the same way. The pads or shoes are pressed against the discs or drums and the friction generated slows the bike. It also wears away the friction material left on the pads or shoes. If too much material is removed, then the brakes may overheat and work less effectively. If all the friction material is allowed to wear away so that the backing plate is exposed, damage will be caused to the discs or drums, which may then need to be replaced.

Checking for wear
Most brake pads have wear indicators that can be checked without the need to remove the calipers. Drums may also have indicators, although in some cases they are more difficult to inspect and can require the wheel to be removed.

Replacing brake pads
Replacing disc brake pads is fairly straightforward, involving removing the calipers and pushing the pistons back with

Brake discs must be above the minimum specified thickness and must be unwarped or the brakes will judder

Check the brake fluid level regularly, and make sure it is replaced in line with the service schedule

a piece of wood to make room for the thicker new pads. Always clean the pistons with brake cleaner to avoid dirt and brake dust being drawn back into the caliper, as this can stop the pistons moving properly.

As the pistons are pushed back in, the brake fluid level may rise, and it may be necessary to siphon some off to prevent spillage. Be careful not to let fluid get on paintwork or plastics, or it may quickly damage the finish.

Once the new pads are fitted, pump the brake lever to press them up against the disc. Make sure the brake fluid level is not too low, or you may allow air to enter the system. Check the brake fluid level before riding and top it up with the correct specification of fluid if necessary.

Brake maintenance

Hydraulic disc systems are self-adjusting, which means that as the pads wear, fluid will be taken from the reservoir into the brake lines. If the level drops below the minimum marked on the reservoir, air can be drawn into the system, giving a spongy feel to the brakes and reducing their effectiveness. If this happens, the brakes will need to be bled. Keep an eye on the fluid level indicators and never let the level drop below the minimum mark. Inspect hoses, seals and unions regularly for signs of leaks and corrosion. Brake fluid absorbs water over time, reducing its efficiency, and it must be replaced at the manufacturer's specified intervals.

In a drum brake system, as the brake shoes wear, it will be necessary to take up slack in the cables and brake rods. Check your Haynes Manual for details of your system.

Discs and drums will need replacing when they become worn. Keep an eye on the surfaces of the brake discs. Over time the metal will wear away and once past the specified minimum (normally stamped on the disc) the disc will need replacing. A warped disc may reveal itself by a judder when applying the brakes and again this means a replacement disc is required. **139**

Cables

Although they are being replaced to some extent by hydraulic and electrical systems, cables are still commonly used to operate a range of components on most bikes – and it is essential to ensure that they operate correctly.

Chafing

A common problem with cables is chafing. The cable flexes when the handlebars are turned and wears through the outer casing. Once the casing is damaged, water gets in, corrosion begins to take hold and the cable action stiffens up and ultimately fails.

Try to spot where chafing may be taking place before it becomes an issue. You should be able to see potential problems by turning the handlebars from lock to lock and observing where the cables may be catching. Flat spots in the cable indicate where they may be chafing.

Trouble can also result when the nipple at the end of a cable seizes up so it is not able to rotate when the lever is applied. When replacing a damaged cable, clean the hole in the lever and smear the nipple with grease to prevent this from happening again.

Cables generally get stiffer to use as they age. This may be due to fraying internally, in which case the cable will need replacing. But if it is simply caused by the build-up of dirt inside the cable then it may be possible to extend the life of the cable by lubricating it.

Controls such as the clutch which are operated by a cable need regular lubrication to work smoothly

A pressure lubricator makes the job of oiling cables quick and easy

Routing problems

Cables should run as straight as possible. If there are tight bends in a cable, it will be harder to operate, and may wear faster inside and start to stick.

If a cable is not properly routed then it may operate when it isn't meant to, because of flexing when the handlebars are turned or the suspension extends and compresses. This is a particular problem on throttle and brake cables.

When you replace a damaged cable, take note of how it is routed before you remove it, so you can ensure that the replacement runs along exactly the same route. Once you have fitted the new cable, turn the handlebars from lock to lock to make sure that it won't operate inadvertently.

Excessive heat can damage a cable, so make sure that cables are routed well away from components that run hot, such as the exhaust pipe.

Adjusting cables

It is important to keep cables properly adjusted so that the controls work as they should do. Your Haynes Manual will give details of how to adjust cables correctly.

Most cables have a barrel and locknut which can be simply turned to adjust the cable. For cable clutches, front brakes and some throttle cables, there is usually one adjuster that provides a large amount of movement at the far end of the cable, and knurled wheel adjusters at the lever ends which can be turned to give fine adjustment. Use these fine adjusters to compensate as the cable stretches with use.

Lubrication

To lubricate a cable thoroughly it is necessary to force the lubricant right through the cable. You can connect an aerosol to an adaptor that seals the end of the cable and squirt the lubricant down the cable, or hand-operated pressure lubricators are available. Use a silicone spray, not oil, if the inner cable has a nylon liner, as oil could cause the liner to swell up and make the cable seize.

Oil changing

The oil in your bike's engine plays a vital role by reducing friction between moving parts, allowing them to operate with minimal wear – but to do its job it must be kept topped up and clean.

Checking the oil

As part of your weekly maintenance routine, check your bike's engine oil level. This will be visible through the oil inspection window on the side of the engine – the oil level should be between the minimum and maximum marks. On some bikes, you will need to check a dipstick. First wipe the oil off the dipstick using a clean cloth, and look for the oil level markings on the bottom end of the dipstick. Push the dipstick slowly all the way back in, then pull it out again and check the oil level. The level should be between the upper and lower marks.

In either case, if the level is near the lower mark, you need to top up the oil. Remove the oil filler cap and pour in a little oil. A funnel will help to avoid spills. Wait a few seconds for the oil to drain down to the bottom of the engine, then re-check the oil level. If the level is still below the upper mark, repeat the topping-up procedure until the level reaches it.

Don't overfill the engine with oil, as this can cause leaks and possibly damage. When you've finished, refit the filler cap tightly, wipe away any spills, and make sure that the dipstick is pushed all the way back into its tube.

Check the engine oil level at regular intervals and top up if needed

It's best to fit a new filter every time you change the oil

Oil change

Oil deteriorates with age, and it needs to be replaced at the intervals recommended by your bike's manufacturer. This is a relatively simple task that you may like to tackle for yourself.

With the engine warm, remove the oil filler cap from the top of the engine. Place a container beneath the engine and slacken the drain plug in the sump using the spanner or drain plug key. Unscrew it by hand the last couple of turns, keeping the plug pressed into its hole. When the plug comes out, pull it away quickly so that the oil runs straight into the container. Most drain plugs are magnetised to collect any small pieces of metal inside the sump, so carefully clean the plug and replace the old sealing washer with a new one. When the oil stops draining, wipe around the drain plug hole, then screw in the plug and tighten it.

Most bikes larger than 125cc have an oil filter, which may be located externally or internally. Most external filters screw on, and can be slackened off with a socket strap tool. Once the filter is loose, unscrew it by hand. Drain the oil from inside the filter into the container. Wipe clean the filter mounting on the engine. Take the new oil filter and, using your finger, smear a little clean engine oil on the rubber sealing ring before screwing it into place. Do not over tighten the filter.

Remove the draining container and pour the old oil into a container to take to your local oil recycling centre.

Check your handbook to see how much oil the engine needs, then pour in about two-thirds of this through the filler hole. Wait a few minutes for the oil to drain down into the engine, then check the oil level. Keep topping up the oil and re-checking the level until the level reaches the maximum mark, then refit the filler cap.

Start the engine and check that the oil pressure warning light goes out. Run the engine for a few minutes and check for leaks around the oil filter and drain plug. Re-tighten slightly if necessary, but don't over tighten. Stop the engine and wait a few minutes for the oil to run down into the sump again, then re-check the oil level and top up if necessary.

143

Cooling system

Motorbikes produce heat when they run. The heat building up in the engine must be dispersed by an effective cooling system, or the engine will overheat and suffer expensive damage.

Motorbike engines are either air-cooled or liquid-cooled. Air-cooling is the more straightforward system. The engine is surrounded with metal cooling fins. As the bike moves along, the air flows over these fins and takes away the heat with it. Some have an additional oil radiator, so the oil can play a bigger part in dispersing excess heat.

Liquid-cooling is more popular these days, but it's also more complicated. In a liquid-cooled engine, coolant is pumped through the engine. Heat transfers from the engine to the coolant which flows through a radiator where it is cooled. It is essential that the coolant keeps flowing, or the engine will start to overheat.

Thermostat

The thermostat is a vital element in the cooling system. When the engine starts from cold, the thermostat is closed and keeps the coolant circulating within the engine. Once the coolant heats up, the thermostat opens and allows the coolant to flow to the radiator.

A faulty thermostat can cause trouble in two ways. If it sticks open, then coolant flows to the radiator even when it is cold, and the engine takes too long to warm to its correct operating temperature. If the thermostat sticks closed, then the coolant cannot get to the radiator and the engine will overheat.

Check that the level in the coolant reservoir is between the 'FULL' and 'LOW' lines

If the coolant level is low, top up with the recommended coolant mixture

If the thermostat appears to be faulty, you will need to remove it and check it is working correctly. At room temperature, the thermostat should be closed – if it remains open then it has failed. If you heat the thermostat in a pan of water it should open. Check that the temperature at which it opens matches the figure specified in your Haynes Manual.

Radiator

Check the radiator and associated hoses regularly for signs of leaks or damage. If the radiator gets clogged by debris it will lose efficiency. Clean it by forcing water from a hose through the fins in the opposite direction to the air flow.

To provide more cooling in hot weather or when the bike is stationary or running at a low speed, an electric fan fitted to the radiator switches on to pull through extra air. The fan is operated by a temperature sensor, which starts the fan when the coolant reaches a set temperature.

If the fan fails to come on, or if it comes on too early or stays on all the time, then it is likely that the temperature sensor is faulty (though check the fuse first, if the fan doesn't work at all).

Coolant

In order to do its job correctly, engine coolant must be kept at the right level. As part of your regular maintenance routine, check that the coolant level is between the maximum and minimum levels marked on the coolant reservoir. Top it up with the correct mixture if it falls below the minimum level.

When topping up, mix water with the recommended amount of anti-freeze. If you use plain water on its own, and the bike is exposed to sub-zero temperatures, then the cooling system will freeze and suffer leaks or more serious engine damage. Anti-freeze also contains corrosion inhibitors which help keep the cooling system healthy.

Bearings

Your motorbike is fitted with bearings which allow components to move freely and smoothly. They need to be maintained and checked regularly for signs of wear.

There are three sets of bearings which need to be checked – wheel, suspension and steering bearings.

Wheel bearings

The wheel bearings allow the wheels to rotate smoothly. They are usually ball-type bearings, one pressed into each side of the hub. Chain-driven bikes often have a third bearing in the rear-wheel sprocket carrier assembly. Shaft-driven bikes may have an extra bearing or bearings in the bevel mechanism of the shaft drive.

Worn front-wheel bearings are the likely cause if you hear any roughness or grinding when the wheel rotates. You can also check to see if there is any sideplay. Doing this is easier if you have an assistant who can help you by holding the front wheel off the ground. If you have a centre stand, ask your helper to press on the back of the bike until the front wheel is raised free. On a bike without a centre stand, your helper will need to lean the bike over on its side stand until its front wheel is clear of the ground.

Once the front wheel is raised, take hold of it from one

Any roughness in the steering means the bearings need to be checked

side and pull the top towards you while simultaneously pushing the bottom of the wheel away. Check for sideplay, and listen for any clicks or clunks which indicate that the bearings are in need of replacement.

Carry out the same procedure for the rear wheel, again preferably with the bike on its centre stand so the wheel can be raised off the ground.

Suspension bearings

There are bearings on the rear suspension and swingarm. If these have greasing points, then lubricate them at the intervals laid down in your bike's maintenance schedule to prevent premature wear.

As with the wheel bearings, you need to move the swingarm from side to side to check that its bearings are sound. Again, you will need the help of an assistant who can help you to do this with the bike on its stand with its rear wheel raised off the ground. There are various different types of swingarm bearing, so refer to your Haynes Manual for details on how to replace them.

On monoshock bikes, check for play in the bearings or bushes. With the rear wheel off the floor and no weight on the swingarm, pull the top of the rear wheel upwards and check for untoward noises or free play.

Steering bearings

If the steering head bearings become worn it can cause the bike to weave and wobble. Regular greasing and correct adjustment will help to maintain them in good condition.

To check these bearings, raise the front wheel off the ground and move the handlebars from side to side. (If a steering damper is fitted, wind this off to its lowest setting.) The steering should feel smooth and light, with no notchiness.

Check also that the bearings are correctly adjusted. With the front wheel raised, ask your assistant to push and pull the bottom of the fork legs, while checking for any movement between the back of the top yoke and front of the fuel tank. If you feel any movement, it indicates that the bearings are loose and in need of adjustment.

147

Tyre care

Tyres are what keep your motorbike on the road, so you need to make sure that you keep them in tip-top condition.

It is essential for your safety that your bike's tyres are looked after. Get in the habit of glancing at your tyres every time you use your bike to check for obvious defects such as cuts, bulges, or glass or nails stuck in the tread.

Tyre pressures
Every week check that your tyres are at your bike manufacturer's recommended pressures. If you are riding with a pillion or luggage, check your manual as it may recommend different pressures than when riding solo and unladen.

After checking the pressures, remember to replace the valve caps. Valves can lose air as the tyre rotates at speed if the cap is missing. Metal caps with rubber seals inside are best for motorbikes.

Tread condition
Look on your tyres for wear indicators. These are small raised sections in the bottom of the tread grooves. When the tread wears down to the level of these indicators, the tyre has reached the end of the manufacturer's recommended safe wear limit.

The legal tread depth requirement for motorbike tyres is at least 1.0mm of tread forming a continuous band across at least three-quarters of the width of the tyre and all the way around the tyre. But you should regard this as the absolute

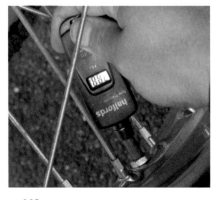

Check tyre pressures regularly to keep your bike safe and prevent unnecessary tyre wear

Replace a tyre when the tread is level with the wear indicator

minimum. Worn tyres greatly reduce roadholding on damp, flooded or icy roads, and for safety's sake you should start thinking about replacing a tyre well before it reaches the legal limit, especially if you intend riding through the winter.

Rear tyres tend to wear out before the fronts as they do the hard work of transmitting power to the road.

A tyre may need replacing before it is worn out if it suffers damage such as a puncture, or a cut that is longer than 25mm or 10% of the width of the tyre and deep enough to reach the ply.

In some cases punctures on tubeless tyres can be repaired using mushroom type plugs, depending on the size of the hole and where it is located. Puncture repair is not permitted when the damage is on the sidewall rather than the tread.

Tyres also sometimes need replacing if they 'square off' and lose their semi-circular profile, something that can happen if your daily commute takes in few corners.

Tyre fitting

Tyres are tested in pairs, so when buying a new tyre don't be tempted to mix different tyres front and rear. Don't buy wider than standard tyres either – they are more likely to upset the handling than provide more grip. Always fit tyres of the correct load and speed ratings for your bike.

When fitting new tyres, it's best to visit a tyre fitter as it's important to get wheels balanced accurately after replacing a tyre. Unbalanced wheels can upset the handling of a bike and cause premature tyre wear.

Tyre valves can harden and perish with age, so it makes sense to have new valves fitted to the wheel rims when having new tubeless tyres fitted. Some tyres are marked with coloured dots to indicate the lightest part of the tyre, and this must be positioned by the valve. Tyres should always be fitted in the direction of travel as indicated by an arrow on the tyre.

If replacing a tyre with an inner tube, make sure a new tube is fitted along with the replacement tyre.

Electrics

Faults with the electrical system are a common cause of problems on bikes. A little bit of care will ensure they keep operating smoothly and avoid a frustrating breakdown.

Battery

A quick battery check each week can help to avoid trouble – faulty battery connections and flat batteries are among the most common causes of breakdowns.

Check that the cable clamps are tight to ensure good connections – you shouldn't be able to move them. Also check the battery cables for cracks and fraying.

If the cable clamps are corroded with white fluffy deposits, clean them with a small wire brush. Corrosion can be prevented by spraying the terminals with battery terminal protector or smearing them with petroleum jelly.

Most modern batteries are maintenance-free and don't need to be topped up. Otherwise, you need to check the battery is filled to within the levels indicated on the casing. If it's low, top it up with a little de-ionised water, being careful not to get any acid from the battery on you or the bike. If the battery needs frequent topping up it may mean that there is a problem with the charging system.

Connectors

Push-fit connectors can fail if moisture gets inside them. To prevent this, split the connector and spray a little contact cleaner onto the pins. A squirt of WD40 on the connector body will make it easier to split next time and help keep out the damp.

Check regularly that all the lights are working, including indicators and brake light

Sometimes fuses just fail for no apparent reason – but if they fail again after replacement it indicates a more serious fault

Ignition problems

Signs of a problem include engine misfiring when accelerating, and difficulty starting the engine, especially in damp weather. To help avoid problems, new spark plugs should be fitted at the manufacturer's recommended intervals. Check also that the HT leads that connect the spark plugs to the ignition coil are clean and securely connected.

Lights

Check regularly that all the lights, including brake lights and indicators, are working properly. Lights on some bikes are prone to failing due to high levels of vibration. The indicators should flash between one and two times per second. If the signal warning light starts flashing quicker than usual, it usually means that one of the indicator bulbs has failed.

After checking the lights, remember to sound the horn to make sure that it's working too.

Fuses

If any item of electrical equipment stops working, the first thing to check is its fuse. Make sure you know where your bike's fuse box is located – often under the seat or beneath the fairing. Some small bikes have just a single fuse for all the electrical systems, usually located near the battery.

A fuse may blow for no obvious reason, in which case you can simply replace it and the problem is solved. But if the fuse blows again in quick succession, it means there's a short circuit or a fault with the electrical component which will need investigating and rectifying.

Switches

Handlebar switches are especially exposed to the elements and it's a good idea, once a year, to remove the switches, clean away any corrosion and apply a smear of petroleum jelly to the switch components.

151

Storing your bike

Many riders take their bikes off the road when the cold wet days of winter arrive. But there's more to storing a bike than just wheeling it into the garage and leaving it there.

Clean it first

If you put away your bike damp and covered with road salt then corrosion will continue to eat away at it while it is stored. So first give your bike a good wash. Remove the fairing so you can get at all those hard to reach nooks and crannies. The cleaning process can be speeded by using a pressure washer, but take care to avoid forcing water into bearings or electrical connections and components.

Having cleaned it, you must make sure your bike is completely dry before putting it into storage. Run the engine until it is hot, then allow to cool, before covering it up. Oil the chain, and spray a light coating of WD40 onto exposed metal and chrome parts, including wheel rims and fork sliders.

Once you have put your bike away it is not a good idea to start it up periodically. Unless the engine is allowed to get really hot, this is likely to cause condensation to form inside the engine and exhaust, which can encourage corrosion.

Engine

Ensure that the piston bores and rings are protected by a layer of oil by removing the spark plugs and squirting a teaspoon of oil down each spark plug hole. Replace the plugs and crank

Secure a polythene bag over the exhaust to prevent condensation

Disconnect the battery and put it on a trickle charger while your bike is in storage

the engine using the kickstart, or on the electric start with the kill-switch off.

If your bike has a liquid-cooled engine, check it is filled with anti-freeze at the correct concentration. This not only prevents the system from freezing and causing expensive damage, but the anti-freeze also contains a corrosion inhibitor.

To help prevent condensation forming, plug the air intake and exhaust pipe or cover them in polythene.

Fuel system

Turn off the fuel tap and run the engine until it stops. This drains the fuel from the system and prevents sticky petrol residue from building up. Better still, drain the petrol out completely. Turn off the fuel tap and open the drain screws at the bottom of the carburettor float bowls.

Petrol can go off if left in a fuel tank for a long time, so consider adding fuel stabiliser to the petrol. If you drain the fuel tank, there is a risk that it may corrode internally. So either spray the inside of the tank with WD40, or remove it, pour in half a litre of engine oil and shake the tank until its interior is thoroughly coated with oil. Remember to clean the oil out before you refill the tank with petrol.

Battery

Remove your bike's battery and store it where there is no danger of it freezing. Make sure that the battery is topped up to the correct level, and use a trickle charger to maintain its charge over the winter months.

Tyres

Leaving your bike standing on flat tyres all winter can cause them to lose their shape, forming a flat spot at the bottom, or even to split. If your bike has a centre stand, raise it on that and rotate the wheels every so often so that they don't spend too long standing on one section of tyre – or better still, store the bike on paddock stands so that its wheels are kept off the ground.

Security

Motorbikes are sadly vulnerable to theft. More than one in five vehicles stolen is a motorcycle. So what can you can do to reduce the chance of your bike being the target of thieves?

Lock it up

Around half of the motorbikes that get stolen do not have security locks fitted. So no matter how short a time you intend to leave your bike unattended, always lock it up. A disc lock or U-lock can be fitted through the brake disc to prevent the wheel turning. These have the advantage of being easy to carry on the bike. They provide an element of visible deterrent, hopefully enough to deter casual theft. But these locks can't prevent a professional thief lifting your bike bodily into a van and driving off with it.

To combat this, you need a strong padlock and chain with which to secure your bike to an immovable object and prevent it being moved. While providing more security, these have the disadvantage of being more awkward to carry. You should never carry a lock and chain around your waist or over your shoulder while you are riding.

Make sure when locking your bike that you don't thread the chain through a part of the bike that can be easily removed. In the case of the wheels, wrap the chain round the rim, not through the spokes which could be cut to release the bike. Make sure also not to leave too much slack in the chain. If a thief can rest the lock or chain on the ground he will find it much easier to break it open with a hammer.

Fit a wheel lock as the first line of deterrence against bike thieves

Many insurance companies offer a discount if you fit an alarm/immobiliser

Alarms and immobilisers

Alarms and immobilisers provide an extra level of protection. They cost more than a simple lock, but many insurance companies offer a discount if you fit one.

For a more expensive bike, you could consider getting a tracking system installed. A covert transmitter hidden in the bike activates when it is stolen and sends out a signal which the police can follow to recover it – hopefully arresting the culprits at the same time.

Secure parking

Whenever you park your bike, look for somewhere well-lit with plenty of passers-by, where a thief will be less able to work undetected.

Always use bike anchors wherever they are provided in parking areas. Putting a cover over your bike can help to conceal it – and the scruffier the cover, the less a thief will be likely to suspect that there is something worth stealing hidden underneath it.

Although you may feel your bike is safe at home, in fact most bike thefts occur from their owner's home. Look after your bike keys, and don't leave them near the front door where a thief can break in and take them.

The safest place to store your bike is in a locked shed or garage. For extra security, fit a ground anchor and lock your bike securely to it. Put some extra security deadlocks on your garage door too, as the standard lock is unlikely to deter a determined thief.

Almost three-quarters of stolen bikes are broken up to be sold for spare parts. You can help to combat this by using a tagging system such as Datatag. Tagging uses numbers, microdots or microchip tags stamped on to the bike's components. These codes allow the owner to be traced and contacted when the stolen parts are located by the police.

Index

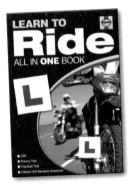

Whatever your area of interest, Haynes have got it covered...

From car service and repair manuals covering 95% of cars on the roads today, to techbooks and restoration manuals...

...service and repair manuals for motorcycles ranging from superbikes to scooters and motorcycle techbooks...

...books for cyclists feature *The Bike Book* and *Mountain Biking Skills*...

...books for the home including the *Washing Machine Manual, Loft Conversion Manual* and home repairs...

...books for travelling, including *The Caravan Manual* and *Driving Abroad* and, last but not least, books for reading and enjoying...

...Motorsport biographies, Formula 1, motorcycling, classic cars, and much, much more...